The Amazonian "Other"

This book explores representations of Amazonian Indigenous peoples in contemporary cultural texts. It analyzes a variety of mediums from novels and films to games and exhibitions, uncovering a distorted image of Indigenous peoples of the Amazon in Euro-American common imagination. The author suggests that these texts rely on a stereotypical vision that was shaped in the first decades of colonization. The chapters consider the formation of the image of Amazonian Indigenous people throughout history and some of the contemporary issues they face, touching on daily life and themes such as shamanism and cannibalism. Together they highlight the misrepresented image of Indigenous groups in the Amazon, who are portrayed as different, even strange, in relation to Western culture. The argument put forward is that both "exotic" and "self-exoticization" rely on the notion of otherness, leading to romanticization, patronization, and caricature. The book will be of particular interest to scholars of Indigenous studies, Latin American studies, cultural studies, anthropology, and comparative literature.

Aleksandra Wierucka is Assistant Professor in the Department of Cultural Studies at the University of Gdańsk, Poland.

The Amazonian "Other"
Representations of Indigenous Peoples in Contemporary Cultural Texts

Aleksandra Wierucka

LONDON AND NEW YORK

First published in English 2025
by Routledge
4 Park Square, Milton Park, Abingdon, Oxon OX14 4RN

and by Routledge
605 Third Avenue, New York, NY 10158

Routledge is an imprint of the Taylor & Francis Group, an informa business

© 2025 Aleksandra Wierucka

The right of Aleksandra Wierucka to be identified as author of this work has been asserted in accordance with sections 77 and 78 of the Copyright, Designs and Patents Act 1988.

All rights reserved. No part of this book may be reprinted or reproduced or utilised in any form or by any electronic, mechanical, or other means, now known or hereafter invented, including photocopying and recording, or in any information storage or retrieval system, without permission in writing from the publishers.

Trademark notice: Product or corporate names may be trademarks or registered trademarks, and are used only for identification and explanation without intent to infringe.

Published in Polish by TAiWPT Universitas 2020

British Library Cataloguing-in-Publication Data
A catalogue record for this book is available from the British Library

ISBN: 978-1-032-77672-9 (hbk)
ISBN: 978-1-032-80023-3 (pbk)
ISBN: 978-1-003-49505-5 (ebk)

DOI: 10.4324/9781003495055

Typeset in Times New Roman
by Apex CoVantage, LLC

Contents

1	Introduction	1
2	Stereotype and exoticization	4
3	Shaping the image of Amazonian Indigenous people	7
4	The tropical forest as a living environment	87
5	Conclusions	104
	Index	*109*

1 Introduction

Members of the world's Indigenous cultures have faced a challenging situation for several centuries, encompassing their cultural practices, as well as their economic, social, and political circumstances. The expansion of Western culture, driven by notions of "growth and development", the propagation of religion, and the acquisition of new lands, has brought about significant transformations in the lives of Indigenous populations across nearly every continent. South America, including its Amazon region, is no exception to this historical trend. Since the outset, its inhabitants have been portrayed through lenses of difference, resulting in distorted perceptions of their cultural practices. This image persisted for centuries, despite emerging 20th-century theoretical perspectives such as postcolonialism and posthumanism.

The theories evolved independently of prevailing beliefs and customs, and cultural texts depicting the Indigenous inhabitants of the Amazon region clung to the image crafted in the initial decades after the discovery of the New World. In most of these texts, these people were portrayed as exotic, with this aspect typically emphasized.

The dynamics of the 21st century are poised to alter this situation for several reasons. First, in 2001, the United Nations (UN) proclaimed the Universal Declaration of Cultural Diversity, recognizing cultural diversity as a shared heritage of humanity (UNESCO 2001). Six years later, the United Nations Declaration on the Rights of Indigenous Peoples came into effect (UNESCO 2007), establishing a universal framework of minimum standards for the survival, dignity, and well-being of Indigenous peoples worldwide. The mere creation of such a declaration underscores the challenging life situation of local inhabitants representing a culture different from the dominant one in their respective countries. The second reason for anticipating a shift in the perception of Indigenous peoples in the 21st century is their increased engagement in the economic and political arena. Indigenous peoples' actions to defend their rights, enshrined in constitutions or international law, have gained widespread attention (e.g., Crouch 2016). The third reason lies in the development of communication technologies, which have facilitated the dissemination of information about the activities of institutions and local residents advocating

DOI: 10.4324/9781003495055-1

for Indigenous rights. All activities organized by institutions advocating for the rights of Indigenous peoples, as well as those initiated by local residents themselves, are currently widely publicized through various media channels, with a primary focus on social media and independent media. Although some information can also be obtained from mainstream media, this is not a common occurrence. One might assume that the abundance of information available in the modern world would significantly impact our understanding of the "otherness" of Indigenous people. Regrettably, this is not the case. The situation is similar in the Amazon region – issues related to the protection of the Amazon Basin reach the general public, albeit sporadically, through the involvement of celebrities such as Sting (Amazon Watch 2003), Roger Waters (Amazon Watch 2017), or Leonardo DiCaprio (Scott 2019).

Despite these factors, public perception has been slow to change, especially in the context of the Amazon region. Events like the extensive fires in July and August 2019 drew attention due to their magnitude, covering almost one-third of the Amazon rainforest (Borunda 2019). However, comprehensive information about South America is scarce unless it relates to political or economic developments. This makes it challenging to form a complete picture of the tropical forest and its inhabitants based on fragmented and temporary information.

The research leading to this book originated from a sense of frustration. Many contemporary Western cultural texts featuring Amazonian characters often relegate them to an attractive, "exotic" backdrop rather than as key characters. It seemed that discussions about the plight of Indigenous groups in the Amazon region and their activities were not reaching the general public. Most cultural texts, including books, films, and art exhibitions, appeared impervious to the evolving world and the challenges faced by people from Indigenous cultures. This frustration prompted an investigation into whether the portrayal of Amazonian inhabitants in 21st-century cultural publications is based on stereotypes established in Western culture long ago or if any changes have occurred. The past two decades appear to be a critical juncture for such potential transformations.

In the research process, I analyzed texts related to cultures of the Amazon region, assumed to be fictional, including literature for children and youth, feature films, artistic photo exhibitions, video games, or theater performances. While documentaries, reports, biographical books, or travel books influence the perception of Indigenous inhabitants of the Amazon rainforest, I excluded them from consideration due to their different purposes.

My focus was on understanding how artistic texts portray the inhabitants of the Amazon region, examining the images they create and the extent to which they adhere to Western patterns. While it's impossible to encompass all cultural texts created in the last 20 years, the selection in this book results from years of research, discussions, and assistance from friends, comprising over 60 texts that have reached a wider audience within Western culture. Some texts, due to their local distribution, completed availability, or temporary nature, were inaccessible.

Within the presented group of cultural texts, I sought the underlying message regarding the Indigenous inhabitants of the Amazon valley, avoiding traditional reviews. Instead, I extracted elements from these works that shape the image of the region. The analysis involved comparing artistic elements with the reality of Indigenous groups, revealing the relationship between the created image and the actual one. This juxtaposition sometimes placed high and popular culture works side by side, emphasizing the cultural key over the form of the analyzed text.

The book's structure mirrors the research process, commencing with discussions on the concepts of "other", stereotype, and exoticism, forming the foundation for the subsequent analysis of cultural texts. A presentation of the historical shaping of the Amazon inhabitants' image is deemed necessary for interpreting contemporary cultural texts. Five key categories emerged from the overall examination: everyday life, shamanism, cannibalism, contemporary issues, and the tropical forest as a living environment. These categories provide a framework for the argument.

It is important to clarify the rule I adopted when defining the groups discussed. "Amazonian peoples" or "Indigenous inhabitants of the Amazon region" are understood as groups that inhabited the Amazon valley before European arrival. Due to the complex and diverse societies resulting from colonization processes, this definition emphasizes the groups covered by the analysis.

References

Amazon Watch. (2003). https://amazonwatch.org/news/2003/0904-hollywood-stars-rally-for-the-rainforest (accessed 12.12.2023).

Amazon Watch. (2017). https://amazonwatch.org/news/2017/1012-us-and-them-affected-peoples-vs-chevron-in-canada (accessed 12.12.2023).

Borunda, A. (2019). See How Much of the Amazon Is Burning, How It Compares to Other Years. *National Geographic*, August 29. https://www.nationalgeographic.com/environment/article/amazon-fires-cause-deforestation-graphic-map (accessed 20.12.2023).

Crouch, D. (2016). Sweden's Indigenous Sami People Win Rights Battle Against State. *The Guardian*, 3 March 2016. https://www.theguardian.com/world/2016/feb/03/sweden-indigenous-sami-people-win-rights-battle-against-state (accessed 26 February 2020).

Scott, K. (2019). Leonardo di Caprio Fund Donating $5M to Help Quell Amazon Fires. *Global News*. https://globalnews.ca/news/5814841/leonardo-dicaprio-find-donate-5m-amazon-fires/ (accessed 12.03.2024).

UNESCO. (2001). unesco.org/en/ev.php-URL_ID=13179&URL_DO=DO_TOPIC&URL_SECTION=201.html,art.2 (accessed 21 March 2020).

UNESCO. (2007). https://www.un.org/development/desa/indigenouspeoples/declaration-on-the-rights-of-indigenous-peoples.html (accessed 26 February 2020).

2 Stereotype and exoticization

The distinction between "stranger" and "other" is based on a change in the speaker's attitude – "stranger" is hostile, whereas "other" acknowledges the differences of the other person on equal terms. In anthropology, which is a very young science, these terms are often used interchangeably, but in philosophy until the 18th century, foreigners were represented as "wild". However, this term did not necessarily mean something offensive – the "savage" was associated with the adjective "noble", and this originated in John Dryden's tragedy from 1672, where the term "noble savage" was used in the context of a free person close to nature, which could be so before European law reached him (Dryden 1672). The concept of a "noble savage" living in harmony with nature and therefore being able to achieve happiness (unlike the people of Europe living among numerous cultural commands and prohibitions limiting their freedom) became part of Western culture and became one of the possibilities for understanding and interpreting people "strange" to their culture.

In the case of the inhabitants of the Amazon, their "otherness" to Euro-Americans was (and still is) something obvious – from skin tone, through daily practices, to spirituality. The encountered otherness in both Americas became fodder for Eurocentrism as a way of interpreting the world from the early days of colonization.

As Peter Gow writes, during the colonization period, arrivals from Europe and Indigenous peoples became images of otherness in the fullest sense: "gringo" is what the native is not – and conversely, the image of the Native American is an image of what the European is not (Gow 1993: 335). The concept of "stranger" serves as the foundation for constructing an image or understanding of what is considered "other". When a group is unfamiliar, and we possess only fragmentary information about it, various stereotypes emerge to "tame" or categorize it, often leading to misconceptions.

The term "stereotype" was coined by Walter Lippmann in 1922, defining it as a model arising from limited knowledge about the outside world, forming an idea about something or someone (Lippmann 1922). Today, a stereotype is defined as "a cognitive structure encompassing the observer's knowledge, beliefs, and expectations about certain social groups" (Mackie 1999:

DOI: 10.4324/9781003495055-2

40). The process of creating such a structure is influenced by several elements, with categorization being a fundamental factor. Categorization allows a group to be defined separately, stemming from the need for adaptation and self-assessment, often unifying people in a foreign group. Stereotyping influences communication at the individual, group, and intercultural levels, utilizing mechanisms of categorization, ordering, and simplification to assess situations and predict behaviors.

Stereotypical perceptions pertain to groups rather than individuals. Meeting a person from a stereotyped group may alter one's opinion, albeit likely limited to that individual rather than the entire group. As outlined by Craig McGarthy (2002: 2), stereotypes serve three main functions: explaining situations, reducing interpretative effort, and being shared by a group. Stereotypical opinions about a group are disseminated and popularized, becoming ingrained during the process of enculturation, often used automatically and supported by distorted or random information (Macrae et al. 1999: 191–193). Despite modern awareness of stereotypes and their potential impact, they continue to play a significant role in shaping our perception of reality and assessing other groups.

My research is particularly focused on the stereotype that certain groups are deemed "exotic", different from our own in a "strange" and incomprehensible manner. This often applies to Indigenous groups from various parts of the world, given our limited information about them and the substantial differences between their culture and customs and those of the Western world, which are regarded as a standard.

Indigenous inhabitants of the Amazon are frequently portrayed in cultural texts as part of a stereotype closely tied to exoticism. While the details are discussed in another chapter, I wish to reflect on its nature here.

Andrzej Banach traces the origin of the word "exoticism" from the Greek "exo", meaning "beyond", and the French "étrange", meaning "coming from foreign countries" (Banach 1980: 5). However, the definition by Zdzisław Żygulski, describing exoticism as features specific to countries with different climates and civilizations, seems insufficient (Banach 1980: 5). Andrzej Stoff (1997) attempts to differentiate three related concepts: exotics as a culturally different reality, exoticism as a literary category presenting reality in literary works, and exoticness as a psychological category influencing how the world is perceived.

While "exotic" might seem closely related to "alien", the latter carries a potential threat, making "exotic" signify something different, strange, unexpected, and distant. In recent years, a new concept has emerged: exoticization. Originating from Edward Said's orientalism, it narrows down to a way of thinking based on the distinction between the "East" and the "West". Today, exoticism emphasizes elements as exotic, even if they do not necessarily fall into that category, making it an interpretation focusing on exotic elements. This process relies on stereotypes and opinions that may not align with reality.

Exoticization implies the objectification and commodification of the "alien", reducing them to a colorful spectacle. To be "de-exoticized", the exotic "Stranger" must turn into "Other", a challenging task in Western culture. From a Eurocentric perspective, exoticism is the reception of inhabitants from other parts of the world by representatives of European culture. However, it's crucial to recognize that, from the local population's standpoint, a European may also be considered "exotic". Everything culturally distant may appear exotic, but geographical distance makes it easier to exoticize. While the scientific community has moved away from exoticism, cultural practices still often exhibit Eurocentrism, considering everything outside Europe or the broader Euro-American culture as exotic.

In everyday practices, Eurocentrism prevails, evident in inappropriate remarks and jokes about the "exoticity" of inhabitants in remote areas. Bruce Kapferer and Dimitrios Theodossopoulos (2016) argue that both "exoticism" (as a result of colonialism) and "self-exoticization" (arising from a group's adaptation to colonial expectations) depend on otherness and make use of references to it – romanticizing, patronizing, and caricaturing it. This, they claim, is essentially what we encounter in culture, and it is what I attempt to prove in this book.

References

Banach, A. (1980). *O potrzebie egzotyzmu*. Wydawnictwo Literackie.
Dryden, J. (1672). The Conquest of Granada by the Spaniards. *Henry Herringman*. https://www.gutenberg.org/files/15349/15349-h/15349-h.htm (accessed 13.03.2019).
Gow, P. (1993). Gringos and Wild Indians: Images of History in Western Amazonian Cultures. *L'Homme*, 33(126/128), 327–347.
Kapferer, B., & Theodossopoulos, D. (eds.). (2016). *Against Exoticism: Toward the Transcendence of Relativism and Universalism in Anthropology*. Berghahn.
Lippmann, W. (1922). *Public Opinion*. Harcourt Brace.
Mackie, D.M. (1999). Social and Psychological Foundations of the Formation of Stereotypes. [in:] *Stereotypes and Prejudices* (Latest edition), ed. C.N. Macrae, Ch. Stagnor, & M. Hewstone. Gdańsk Psychological Publishing Office.
Macrae, C.N. et al. (1999). *Stereotypy i uprzedzenia*. Gdańskie Wydawnictwo Psychologiczne.
McGarthy, C. (2002). Social, Cultural and Cognitive Factors in Stereotype Formation. [in:] *Stereotypes as Explanations*, ed. C. McGarthy, V.Y. Yzerbyt, & R. Spears. Cambridge University Press.
Stoff, A. (1997). Egzotyka, egzotyzm, egotyczność. Próba rozgraniczenia pojęć. [in:] *Studia z teorii literatury i poetyki historycznej*. Towarzystwo Naukowe Katolickiego Uniwersytetu Lubelskiego.

3 Shaping the image of Amazonian Indigenous people

The way of presenting Indigenous people (not only of the Amazon but the whole of South and North America in general) undoubtedly has its source already at the beginning of geographical discoveries and the later colonization of the New World. After the first meeting, Christopher Columbus perceived the local inhabitants rather as an element of nature instead of actual people (Columbus n.d.). According to Tzvetan Todorov (1996: 43), the nudity of the local peoples translated into the lack of culture and, thus, the lack of any values, beliefs, or even customs. Treated as an element of nature, the Indigenous appear as handsome, well-built, etc., but besides that, they are seen as naive and unsophisticated and shortly thereafter as thieves and barbarians (Todorov 1996: 48). All these opinions result from the simple belief in the superiority of Western culture over Indigenous people and therefore also in the superiority of the culture of "explorers" and later colonizers over local cultures. This belief has been around for five centuries and has also influenced how the representatives of Euro-American culture perceive the Indigenous peoples of both American continents today.

The first accounts created the image of the Amazon region, which to some extent is still applicable today, and based on it, the images of the Amazon valley are built: a huge space covered with a network of rivers, the elusive presence of mysterious, and sometimes hostile natives, but at the same time a place of many possible miraculous discoveries – cities made of gold and unknown empires await hidden in the forest (Whitehead 2002: 126).

Stephen Nugent lists several specific phases of the development of accounts about the Amazon area and its inhabitants: the first phase (16th and 17th centuries) concerns descriptions of journeys along the Amazon River made by clergy accompanying soldiers and travelers; the second phase (18th century) is associated with researchers and explorers, and the third phase, with the activities of scientists creating natural and ethnographic collections (19th century); the fourth phase is represented by ethnographers officially collecting data (first half of the 20th century); and in the fifth phase, we are dealing with the opening of the Amazon region through the construction of a trans-Amazon route (Nugent 2007: 71).

DOI: 10.4324/9781003495055-3

8 *Shaping the image of Amazonian Indigenous people*

The first sensational description of the Indigenous inhabitants of the Amazon region appeared relatively early, because already at the beginning of the 16th century (Hemming 1995b: 13), Amerigo Vespucci wrote a letter to Prince Lorenzo Pietro Francesco di Medici in 1503, in which he reported his stay in the colony in 1501–1502. The letter was published soon after and became a bestseller at the time. Vespucci emphasized these features, which are different from European ones, to create a sense of astonishment among the readers. He described, among others, freedom and innocence, as well as the lack of private property or lack of money (Vespucci 1894: 47).[1] The "savagery" of the Indigenous peoples was therefore emphasized in the accounts as a sensation from the very beginning.

Another image of the population inhabiting the Amazon was included in the travel description of Francisco de Orellana, a Spaniard who first sailed the Amazon River between 1541 and 1542, starting from the Napo River (in the area of today's Ecuador) and ending at the mouth of the Amazon River (in the area of today's Brazil) – (Little 2001: 42). Participants of this expedition that went down in history suffered from hunger and weakness, but also from repeated attacks of local residents who lived along the river (Hemming 2008: 24). Some locals, however, accepted strangers as friends and shared food with them, which enabled the Spaniards to survive. All events related to Orellana's journey were documented by his companion, a Dominican, Gaspar de Carvajal.[2] His work was published late, only in the 19th century, but it still had an impact on the idea of the Amazon inhabitants because it showed them just before the actual colonization.

Carvajal described not only the course of the expedition (1934) but also the Indigenous groups encountered. An image of the cultural diversity of the Amazon which was not expected earlier in the area emerges from his work. In addition, three specific facts could be extracted from Carvajal's text: in some parts of the Amazon, the banks are densely populated by organized groups; people are able to source food in this area (while Europeans are struggling with hunger); and many groups remain at war with each other (Hemming 2008: 34). At that time, this constituted valuable information that could be used for further conquest.

For later stereotype of the Amazon people, the Carvajal's work brings an important element: brave Indigenous women living in separate settlements, raising only girls and cutting off their breasts to better shoot from the bow. The Hellenic myth found its embodiment in the Amazon area (Chołaj 1995: 187): the Dominican was convinced that the representatives of this group were encountered during the expedition, but today the researchers claim that it was probably the representatives of the Parikotó or Wai Wai group who tied their long hair high on their heads and thus in combat could seem to be women to Europeans unaccustomed to such views (Chołaj 1995: 33).[3] Nevertheless, the description of Carvajal is associated with the name of warrior women, which came from a collection of popular legends at that time. European travelers were looking for this type of curiosity, and the word "Amazons" was quickly adopted after the Carvajal report as the name of the river. As Hemming writes, the world's largest river was named after a legendary group of sexually liberated women (Hemming 2008: 33).

A hundred years later Cristóbal de Acuña accompanied the Portuguese Pedro Teixeira, who led the first expedition upstream of the Amazon River and the Napo River – travelers left Belém in 1637 and arrived in Quito ten months later. Acuña's description of the groups encountered in the middle course of the river is idyllic, and the author was apparently impressed by the organization of life of the Indigenous groups and their daily resourcefulness (Vieira 2016: 56–57).[4] Many missionaries and travelers of this period made descriptions of peoples encountered in the Amazon region, and some of them certainly made themselves known to the public in Europe.

Numerous accounts of the Indigenous inhabitants of the Amazon present them as "simple", which means easy to convert to Christianity (Vaz de Caminha 1974: 10).[5] However, most of the natives perished before this happened, and the Portuguese in their colony decided that the Indigenous were only fit for slave labor and rape (Rabben 1998: 22). The path from the conviction of simplicity to unequivocal submission was therefore short. The Europeans very quickly obtained an image of an Indigenous, which was far from the truth. Nevertheless, before this image even reached the Old Continent, there were rumors about giants and monsters that supposedly inhabited these areas. This can be evidenced by the account of Jean de Lery, who published his memories of his stay in Brazil in 1578, among the Tupinambá – in the chapter on the appearance of the natives, he writes that "their bodies are not monstrous or huge in relation to ours. In truth, they are stronger, more vigorous . . . and more agile" (de Lery 1990 [1578]: 56). In his narrative, Lery contradicts what perhaps he himself expected and what was then the knowledge in Europe, distorted with distance and lack of reliable information. Simultaneously, Lery emphasizes the bravery of the Indigenous people and their hospitality and puts them on an equal footing with other people questioning the fact of calling them "barbarians" (de Lery 1990 [1578]: 168). Despite Lery's progressive and amicable perspective on the Indigenous peoples of Brazil, it has not resonated widely with the European public. Both the texts of Lery and earlier Bartolomé de las Casas' (1992 [1552]) reached a small group of people, and an untrue image of the Amazon people was created over the next centuries.

This situation was also impacted by the colonial administration of Portugal that managed to maintain a vast colony and did not want to share knowledge about its real or supposed treasures. In the 18th century, travelers and researchers were not allowed to explore the Amazon region, often due to suspicions of espionage. This was the case with Captain Cook in 1768 and Alexander von Humboldt in 1800 (Hemming 1995a: 129), but already in 1808, a Portuguese court arrived in the colony, thanks to which the era of travelers and explorers began soon after (Hemming 1995a: 129). Many of them wrote about their meetings with the locals. Among them was the German prince Maximilian zu Wied-Neuwied, who led the expedition along the banks of the Amazon River and included drawings with scenes of everyday life of locals in his description of the trip. These were the first such illustrations available to readers in Europe (Hemming 1995a: 130). This does not mean, however, that at the beginning of the 19th century the image of the Indigenous inhabitants of other continents was to change. At that time, it was already permanent and differed from reality.

This was influenced not only by excursions but also by their echoes in the literary works of the 16th and 18th centuries. As John Hemming writes, most great thinkers and writers of this period borrowed knowledge from the descriptions of their expeditions to the Amazon Region: among others, in 1516, Thomas Moore placed his Utopia in the New World; in 1533, François Rabelais, while writing "Pantagruel", used the knowledge gained from his friends traveling around the Portuguese colony; Michel de Montaigne studied Lery's works so that in his text he could include a conversation between the Tupinamba and King Charles IX; Daniel Defoe in "Robinson Crusoe" from 1719 introduces cannibalism of Indigenous peoples, and Voltaire in "Candide" has his hero travel through Brazil (Hemming 1995b: 22–23). Therefore, literature along with travel reports shaped the idea of who the Amazon inhabitants were at that time.

More and more Europeans came to the Portuguese colony at the beginning of the 19th century, describing their observations and experiences: for instance, a group of scientists brought in by the fiancée of the Portuguese heir to the throne, the Austrian archduchess Leopoldina (Hemming 1995a: 130). Their opinions about Indigenous peoples of the Amazon region later had significant impact on the perception of the latter in Europe, where new views about man and his place in society developed. This prompted contemplation on the intricate connection between nature and culture, and the concept of the aforementioned "noble savage" has persisted in various forms from that time to the present day (Barnard 2008: 54). However, at the beginning of the 19th century, the Portuguese newcomers perceived Indigenous peoples in a way that also gave the image of the "noble savage" new meaning: in their accounts, the Indigenous are presented as people of a worse category than the educated and enlightened Europeans, and in their personality, features such as laziness and lack of prevention are emphasized (Hemming 1995a: 131). The newcomers were also surprised by the inability to bribe the locals with promises of financial benefits and irritated by their lack of interest in the benefits of "civilization" (Hemming 1995a: 131). This was certainly associated with a complete misunderstanding by the Portuguese (as well as other colonizers) of different Indigenous cultural values. In Europe, opinions have begun to prevail about lazy natives who are interested in nothing but their own stomachs, who have no chance of progressing in the European sense, and who are only capable of submissive work. The "savage" was no longer "noble". In the opinion of Johann B. von Spix and C.F.P. von Martius, German travelers who crossed Brazil,

> Indians cannot stand the higher culture that Europe would like to instil in them. Progressive civilization is a key element in the development of the human community, but it irritates them similarly to destructive poison. In our opinion, they are doomed to extinction, just like other species in the history of nature.
>
> (von Spix 1831)

Similar opinions began to multiply (Hemming 1995a: 135–150) – it was understood that Indigenous peoples could not take care of themselves, that they were lazy, they could not work nor understand European order, etc.

At the end of the 19th century and beginning of the 20th century, three nature explorers, Richard Spruce, Henry W. Bates, and Alfred R. Wallace, arrived in the Amazon rainforest. Descriptions of their expeditions primarily related to the issues of nature in the Amazon River Valley (Bates 1892), but there are also stories about Indigenous groups of the region. The works of biologists were widely read in the Victorian era and reached a large number of recipients, so they also had an impact on the image of the Amazon Indigenous inhabitants in Europe.

In 1853, A. Wallace published a description of his excursion to the Amazon River Valley. It includes, among others, a separate chapter with gathered information on Indigenous people scattered throughout the book. Wallace clearly separates the colonized, partially "culturally deprived" people (living mainly in the eastern regions of Brazil, at the mouths of the Amazon River, whom he describes as calm and having a good nature, who quickly learn the rules of, for example, trade or services in which they often work – Wallace 1889: 332) from those who have still fully preserved their culture. The latter are described in superlatives both in terms of physique (Wallace even defines them as "living illustrations of the beauty of the human form" – Wallace 1889: 332) and culture (the author describes homes, handicrafts, customs, ceremonies, marital practices, economics, leadership structure, and healing practices, but at the same time clearly states that he is unable to determine whether the Indigenous have any spiritual life because they have no idea of God – Wallace 1889: 348). Wallace does not evaluate cultural practices (the author uses the word *peculiar* for detailed data on various previously unknown practices). However, the last sentences in the part describing the Indigenous groups encountered by Wallace match the opinion that prevailed in Europe and in the colonies at that time: "[the indigenous people] seem capable of being formed, by education and good government, into a peaceable and civilised community" (Wallace 1889: 361). In the mid-19th century, despite the observed cultural diversity and appreciation of the cultural practices of the locals, there was no room for reflection on the value that they could bring to the thoughts about humanity.

12 Shaping the image of Amazonian Indigenous people

In 1892, H.W. Bates described the groups he encountered, emphasizing their self-sufficiency, as well as handicraft skills and songs widespread in the area (Bates 1892: ch. IV). As a biologist, he does not pay much attention to what does not belong to the natural world, but the text also contains comments on erroneous opinions about local people, which he managed to personally verify, that is, mainly laziness, practicing theft, cruelty, and the inability to trust (Bates 1892: ch. VII). Bates concludes that it is an exaggeration to define them, as those issues are exaggerated features of the "fundamental defects of the character of Brazilian red people" (Bates 1892: ch. VII). Thus, on the one hand, Bates perceives the wrong approach of other reports regarding Indigenous peoples, but on the other hand, he also remains faithful to the way of thinking about the locals of that time as people of the inferior kind.

The work of the third biologist mentioned above, Richard Spruce, was published in the editorial office of Alfred Wallace in 1908. In 1849–1864, Spruce traveled through Brazil and Peru with local guides, whom he described as lazy and willing to flee their work obligations (Spruce 1908: 23), but also devoted a lot of space to practices related to the use of hallucinogenic drugs (Spruce 1908: 413–455). As a biologist, Spruce was primarily interested in the botanical side of the effect of the hallucinogenic vine *Banisteriopsis caapi* (now commonly known as *ayahuasca*), but he also gives a lot of information about the use of the plant and its consequences. He also mentions the practices of shamans, reducing them to tricks aimed at deceiving the patient (Spruce 1908: 430), at the same time noting that the shaman plays both a spiritual and a medicinal role (Spruce 1908: 433). Spruce also describes the details of herbal practices and the use of various types of plants for everyday ailments, which would confirm his positive opinion on cultural practices – but still, similar to other researchers or travelers of his time, he regarded Indigenous peoples as less advanced in terms of civilization (Spruce 1908: 455).

The views regarding South America, including the Amazon region, were greatly influenced by the works of Alexander von Humboldt, a comprehensive German researcher, whose name is referred to as "the second explorer of America [after Columbus]" (Chołaj 1995: 41). In addition to collecting geographic data, Humboldt was also interested in Americans, he opposed slavery and defended the rights of the locals. His extensive research influenced many different scientific disciplines and shaped science at that time.

In the mid-19th century, photography joined the creators of stereotypical descriptions of Amazonian inhabitants. Readers of accounts could now see the Indigenous people "up close", not only through illustrations but also through photographs, which gradually became more refined over time.

Everard Im Thurn, an English scientist (anthropologist and botanist), a traveler, as well as an employee of the colonial administration, was a person acting at the turn of these two periods and influencing the perception of the Indigenous inhabitants of the Amazon rainforest. In 1877, Im Thurn traveled to Guyana and documented his stay among the Indigenous people for the next few years (Thurn 1883: V). His primary work was published in 1883, and it contained, among others, a description of the population of Guyana, Indigenous languages, cultural practices, or the appearance of Indigenous people and thus constitutes an interesting source of knowledge. The researcher placed great emphasis on photography as a method of showing the cultural context. He claimed that the truthfulness of the photograph is unquestionable (which was not always the case when it comes to drawings – Thurn 1893: 189), but he considered "physiological photography" as the main purpose of using a camera during research, that is, the one that constituted the basis for research of the "alien" at the end of the 19th century:

> An accumulation of a large number of these [photographs] taken in accordance with a fixed scale, would undoubtedly have a very considerable value if, it must be added, these were accompanied by a series of exact measurements of the persons photographed.
>
> (Thurn 1893: 188)

Interestingly, Im Thurn's photographs show local people in artificial poses (e.g., lying on a bed of palm leaves) but Thurn's purpose was not to show the life of local residents, but their bodies in the context of material culture (Nugent 2007: 77).

Nevertheless, according to Nugent, the earliest images depicting the Amazonian Indigenous peoples are a few years younger and date back to around 1860 and were taken by Albert Frisch (Nugent 2007: 89). The subjects in the photographs posed (in the 19th century, there was no other technical possibility), but they capture moments from the people's lives (Nugent 2007: 89–91), which gives them an ethnographic character.

Over the years, the technique of photography evolved and became an integral part of every expedition, not only those with an anthropological focus. Descriptions, along with photographs, gradually solidified the image that had existed since the 17th century, portraying the inhabitants of the Amazon as naked, often armed, aligning with the expectations of the audience.

Film as a new medium soon became intertwined with photography, captivating anthropologists, much like it did with everyone else. The first ethnographic films at the beginning of the 20th century are indistinguishable from "chronicles" that appeared before cinema screenings and also focused on the colonial view of the groups shown (Ruby 2000: 7). From the beginning, there was also a conflict between the commercial and anthropological use of film possibilities (Ruby 2000: 8), which resulted mainly from other goals and technical possibilities. As Jay Ruby writes, historically the ethnographic film did not focus on the possibilities of acquiring research data, but on creating educational aids for teaching anthropology. This was what recordings came down to (Ruby 2000: 8). Many good film ethnographies were created in the 1950s and 1960s – they were directed mainly to university audiences and, more broadly, to viewers of documentary films. "The Hunters" (Marshall 1957) was the first such film shown at festivals portraying Namibian Ju/'hoansi during the hunt for giraffes. Soon after, Timothy Asch, working with anthropologist Napoleon Chagnon (whose influence on the image of the Amazon people is described below), made his famous films (Asch 1968, 1971, 1972), which are still intriguing the audience and are used for educational purposes. Unlike other documentary filmmakers of the time, Asch cooperated with anthropologists, conducted a thorough examination of archives, and assumed that his short productions would constitute a piece of aid to the study of anthropology (Ruby 2000: 133).

Meanwhile, the film industry has developed an interest in the Amazon region, incorporating both its nature and the lives of its inhabitants into popular productions of the 20th century. Besides films that show mostly exaggerated cannibalistic practices, there are also several important productions that go beyond the scheme of depicting the Amazonians as "savage". Interesting items include "The Lost World" (Hoyt 1925), "The Creature from the Black Lagoon" (Arnold 1954), "Aguirre, der Zorn Gottes" (Herzog 1972), "The Emerald Forest" (Boorman 1985b), "Mission" (Joffé 1986), or "Anaconda" (Llosa 1997). The first of these films, "The Lost World" from 1925 directed by Harry O. Hoyt, is a silent adaptation of Arthur Conan Doyle's book with the same title and presents the trip to the Amazon region (Doyle 1912). It is worth noting that the origin of the text on which the film is based: Conan Doyle used Everard Im Thurn's description of his team's ascent to Mount Roraima in Venezuela (Thurn 1885), but the description of nature has been slightly colored, because in the story there are dinosaurs, one of which goes to Europe. Of course, it is not necessary to state how fantastic this image of a tropical forest is. Inhabitants of these areas are also included in the text. We see them as those who are no longer cannibals "directly" but "only" use aliens to feed dinosaurs. As Steven Nugent notes, two types of locals appear in this film: the bad in the "pre-human" form and the good in the form of gentle inhabitants of the highland area (Nugent 2007: 198). The Amazon region presented by Hoyt is based on stereotypes that were already popular at that time and provides the basis for their continuation.

The above "Aguirre, der Zorn Gottes" (Herzog 1972) and "Mission" (Joffé 1986) can be considered as further feature films representative of the image of the Amazon region by being based on historical events. Both show a fairly faithful image of events and Indigenous people, although they are not free from errors, showing, for example, a stereotypical image of the inhabitants of the Amazon (few primitive groups without advanced technology or social structure). Similar effects are not avoided in the film "The Emerald Forest" (Boorman 1985b), although the director in his diary talks about cooperation with specialists in the Amazon (Boorman 1985a). The Amazonian peoples are shown in hyper-reality, which comes mainly from the director's approach as a person with "profound knowledge" about the culture presented (Nugent 2007: 206).

The evolution of both photography and film has resulted in the accessibility for anyone to capture a photo or create a video, subsequently being able to publish it on the Internet and reach a broad audience today. Of course, there are photographs and films that can be called documentaries, and there are also those that are only the result of someone's visit somewhere; however, they create a general image of Indigenous groups (including the Amazonian peoples). When you search the Internet, it turns out that the most commonly found images are of the Amazonians in their "natural" state, that is, naked or dressed only in a loincloth and often holding a gun (the image of the "savage" returns again).[6] Of course, this is influenced by the growth of tourism, because many of these images come from people who have visited the Amazon region and posted their photos and videos online. However, at this point, I will not focus on the issue of the "tourist approach" or satisfying tourist needs, because this topic has already been broadly described (e.g., Hutchins 2007; Greenwood 2004; Urry 1992).

In the reflections on the image of the Amazonian Indigenous peoples, it is impossible to omit the most famous history of research conducted in the 20th century, which entailed far-reaching consequences and had an impact not only the world of science but also the popular opinion about the inhabitants of the rainforest. What I have in mind here are the descriptions of Yanomami groups from the area of modern Brazil and Venezuela. In the past, they were depicted as the least understood groups in the Amazon region, but today, they are among the most well-known and recognized in common awareness. The detailed history of the so-called Yanomami controversy is comprehensively described in the available sources (Albert and Ramos 1989; Bodley 2008; Davis 1976; Borofsky 2005; Ramos and Taylor 1979; Sponsel 2022; Turner 1991 and others), but here I would like to specifically focus on its role in creating the image of the Amazonian peoples.

Napoleon Chagnon's book describing his research in the settlement of Yanomami was one of the first scientific books to become a bestseller (Chagnon 1968). It appeared at a specific time of the development of anthropology in the United States, when it was intensively advancing due to the emergence of new universities, as well as the expansion of research interests beyond the North American continent (Borofsky 2005: 4). In addition to students utilizing his book in anthropological studies, it was widely read across the United States in the early 1970s. The Yanomami culture, like the cultures of other groups in the region, is complex and not based solely on warfare, as Chagnon suggested, while his opinion of the Yanomami warfare as a constituent factor in their culture was taken for granted. This had specific results both for the Indigenous peoples themselves and for research and public opinion. For example, the educational project of Survival International, which is an organization dedicated to helping Indigenous groups, did not receive funding because the UK authorities decided that there was no need to fund projects for a group that does nothing but war.[7] Following Chagnon, research among the Yanomami was conducted by many researchers, and in the meantime, a new word, *anthro* meaning an evil demon, has reportedly appeared in the Yanomami language (Thierney 2001: 14). One of the far-reaching effects of Chagnon's book is the opinion regarding the Yanomami as the "most fierce tribe" in the world. It seems to me that this opinion applies not only to this particular group but also to the Amazonian Indigenous peoples in general.

Notes

1 In the introduction to the publication, Clements R. Markham describes the research, among others, of Bartolomé de las Casas on the credibility of Vespucci's accounts and concludes that *accuracy and truth did not matter. It was about making [readers] believe that Amerigo Vespucci was the discoverer of the New World and its wonders* (Vespucci 1894: XLIII).
2 The Spanish version of Carvajal's report was published in 1894 by J.T. Medina, but only its translation into English reached a wider audience.
3 A.R. Wallace, in his 1853 book, suspects that these were Indians belonging to the Uaupés group (A.R. Wallace 1853: 493).
4 Text by Acuña titled *Nuevo descubrimiento del gran rio de las Amazonas* was published in 1641, but the print was quickly removed. Currently, it is available online: https://archive.org/details/nuevodescubrimi00acugoog/page/n1 (accessed 08.03 2019).
5 Pero Vaz de Caminha was one of the participants of the expedition in 1500 – he wrote a letter to the king of Portugal, in which he described, among others, the local inhabitants he encountered.
6 The image is very similar regardless time of the search for "Amazon Indians" in English. The search for "Amazon Indians" on 11 July 2019 gave 821 million results showing mainly traditional images, often corrected with "natural" underwear made of leaves or red or white materials, blindfolds, hanging rags, "panties", skirts, etc. Situation did not change in 2023 with the search yielding the same image.
7 Information from materials sent by Professor Leslie Sponsel (University of Hawai'i): email exchange, 23 November 2010.

References

Albert, B., & Ramos, A. (1989, May 12). Yanomami Indians and Anthropological Ethics. *Science*, 632.
Arnold, J. (dir.). (1954). *The Creature from the Black Lagoon* [film]. USA.
Asch, T. (1968). *Feast* [film]. USA.
Asch, T. (1971). *The Axe Fight* [film]. USA.
Asch, T. (1972). *A Man Called Bee* [film]. USA.
Barnard, A. (2008). *Antropologia* (S. Szymański, trans.). Państwowy Instytut Wydawniczy.
Bates, H. (1892). The Naturalist on the River Amazons. *D. Appleton*. https://www.gutenberg.org/cache/epub/2440/pg2440-images.html (accessed 22.02.2024).
Bodley, J.H. (2008). *Victims of Progress*. AltaMira Press.

Boorman, J. (1985a). *Money into Light: A Diary.* Faber & Faber.
Boorman, J. (dir.). (1985b). *The Emerald Forest* [film]. Great Britain.
Borofsky, R. (2005). *Yanomami: The Fierce Controversy and What We Can Learn from It.* University of California Press.
Chagnon, N. (1968). *Yanomamö: The Fierce People.* Holt, Rinehart and Winston.
Chołaj, H. (1995). *Kolumb, Europa i świat.* Książka i Wiedza.
Columbus, C. (n.d.). *Extracts from Journal*, 21 October. https://sourcebooks.fordham.edu/source/columbus1.asp (accessed 15.03.2024).
Davis, S.H. (ed.). (1976). *The Geological Imperative: Anthropology and Development in the Amazon Basin of South America.* University of California.
de Carvajal, G. (1934). Carvajal's Account. [in:]. *The discovery of the Amazon according to the account of Friar Gaspar de Carvajal and other documents*, ed. J.T. Medina, trans. J.T. Medina. American Geographical Society.
de las Casas, B. (1992). *A Short Account of the Destruction of the Indies.* Penguin Books.
de Lery, J. (1990). *History of the Voyage to the Land of Brazil, Otherwise Called America* (J. Whatley, trans.). University of California Press.
Doyle, A.C. (1912). *The Lost World.* Hodder & Stoughton.
Greenwood, D.J. (2004). Culture by the Pound: An Anthropological Perspective on Tourism as Cultural Commodity. [in:] *Hosts and Guests. The Anthropology of Tourism*, ed. V.L. Smith. University of Pennsylvania Press, pp. 169–186.
Hemming, J. (1995a). *Amazon Frontier: The Defeat of the Brazilian Indians.* Papermac.
Hemming, J. (1995b). *Red Gold: The Conquest of the Brazilian Indians.* Papermac.
Hemming, J. (2008). *Tree of Rivers: The Story of the Amazon.* Thames & Hudson.
Herzog, W. (1972). *Aguirre, der Zorn Gottes* [film]. Germany-Mexico-Peru.
Hoyt, H. (1925). *The Lost World* [film]. USA.
Hutchins, F. (2007). Footprints in the Forest: Ecotourism and Altered Meanings in Ecuador's Upper Amazon. *Journal of Latin American and Caribbean Anthropology*, 12(1), 75–103.
Joffé, R. (dir.). (1986). *Mission* [film]. Great Britain.
Little, P. (2001). *Amazonia. Territorial Struggles on Perennial Frontiers.* The John's Hopkins University Press.
Llosa, L. (dir.). (1997). *Anaconda* [film]. USA-Brazil-Peru.
Marshall, J. (1957). *The Hunters* [film]. USA.
Nugent, S. (2007). *Scoping the Amazon: Image, Icon, Ethnography.* Left Coast Press.
Rabben, L. (1998). *Unnatural Selection: The Yanomami, the Kayapo and the Onslaught of Civilization.* Pluto Press.
Ramos, A., & Taylor, K. (1979). *The Yanoama in Brazil.* Vol. 37–39. International Work Group for Indigenous Affairs.
Ruby, J. (2000). *Picturing Culture: Explorations of Film and Anthropology.* The University of Chicago Press.

Sponsel, L. (2022). *Yanomami of the Amazon*. Independently Published.
Spruce, R. (1908). *Notes of Botanist on the Amazon and the Andes* (A. Wallace, ed.). Macmillan and Co.
Thierney, P. (2001). *Darkness in El Dorado: How Scientists and Journalists Devastated the Amazon*. Norton & Company.
Thurn, E.I. (1885). The Ascent of Mount Roraima. *Proceedings of the Royal Geographical Society*, 7(8), 497–521.
Todorov, T. (1996). *Podbój Ameryki: Problem innego* (Wojcieszak, J. trans.). Fundacja Aletheia.
Turner, T. (1991). *Report of the Special Commission to Investigate the Situation of the Brazilian Yanomami*. American Anthropological Association.
Urry, J. (1992). The Tourist Gaze and the Environment. *Theory, Culture, Society*, 9(1), 1–26.
Vaz de Caminha, P. (1974). Carta. [in:] *Brazilian Literature 1*, ed. C.L. Hulet. Georgetown University Press.
Vespucci, A. (1894). *The Letters of Amerigo Vespucci and Other Documents Illustrative of His Career* (C.R. Markham, trans.). Burt Franklin.
Vieira, P. (2016, Autumn). Phytofables: Tales of the Amazon. *Journal of Lusophone Studies*, 1(2), 116–134.
von Spix, J.B. (1831). *Riese in Brasilien auf Befehl Sr. Majestät Maximilian Joseph I., Königs van Baiern, in den Jahren 1817–1820* (Vol. 3). Lindauer.
Wallace, A.R. (1853). *A Narrative of Travels on the Amazon and Rio Negro: With an Account of the Native Tribes, and Observations on the Climate, Geology, and Natural History of the Amazon Valley*. Reeve and Co.
Whitehead, N. (2002). South America/Amazonia: The Forest of Marvels. [in:] *The Cambridge Companion to Travel Writing*, ed. P. Hulme, & T. Youngs. University of Cambridge Press.

Presentations in culture-based texts of the 21st century

Throughout the exploration of culture-based texts, five recurring themes have surfaced, offering insights into the typical portrayal of the Indigenous inhabitants of the Amazon. According to the order that appeared in the interpretation, I therefore divided the further work into these five categories: everyday life (most often related to what is visible during the initial contact, what is external), shamanism, cannibalism, contemporary problems, and the tropical forest (as the living environment of Indigenous peoples or as a background of events). The objective was to categorize the discussed culture-based texts in a manner that facilitates an overview of distinct practices, all the while ensuring the continuous examination of topics related to individual cultural groups. In many discussed texts it is possible to find all five of these elements, so it seemed logical to adopt an order that would make them easier to comprehend.

Everyday life

In many cases, separating what is material in culture and what is symbolic is not possible – this is mainly due to the fact that Indigenous cultures do not use a division to the sacred and the secular, known from Western culture. In traditional life, these two spheres intertwine naturally and result from each other. For the sake of an argument, in this part I have handled only those elements of culture that are related to the actual material manifestations of cultural practices: clothing, building houses, ornamentation, or belonging to a group based on the external appearance. The disquisition regarding individual elements has a thematic order – if, for example, there are culture-based texts concerning Yanomami, they are grouped in one thread.

One of the most popular and easily accessible cultural texts concerning the Amazon in recent years is the film "The Lost City of Z" (2016) about the expeditions of Percival Harrison Fawcett, a British military man and traveler. The film is based on David Grann's documentary book (Grann 2009), which is also referred to as "a biography, a detective story and a wonderfully vivid piece of travel writing" (Kakutani 2009). Between 1906 and 1925, Fawcett made three trips to the Brazilian Amazon, led by the conviction that he would be able to find the ruins of an old Indigenous city (the titular "Z") – during his first trip along the Verde River, he came across fragments of decorated ceramics that became his cause for the search. According to the movie announcement, it is based on real events and tells the real story of a search in the Amazon. In addition to the part presenting the expedition, the movie also shows the private life of Fawcett, who left his wife and children three times for several years to carry out his vision. The matter is problematic because at that time, at the beginning of the 20th century, no one believed in the existence of any Indigenous "civilization" – Amazon peoples were considered, as I mentioned earlier, savages incapable of creating anything "higher" from the point of view of Western culture, which is why Fawcett's idea was mocked by the scientific community. After his travels and participation in the First World War, his position increased, and he was awarded the Royal Geographical Society medal and set off on his final expedition together with his eldest son, from which they both did not return – their further fate is unknown.

In "The Lost City of Z", I am interested in the manner of depicting the local people whom the travelers came across. The first scenes including Indigenous peoples present them in an estate of a "rubber baron", because it is still a period of intensively collecting rubber in the Amazon and the film snapshots the dramatic fate of the Indigenous inhabitants – the people are slaves at the service of the land owners. Fawcett gets an Indigenous man as a guide up the river (the purpose of the initial expedition is to find the sources of the Verde River, to establish a border between Bolivia and Brazil due to the growing conflict between these countries). The person is shown as a secretive, silent man who, after leading the expedition to its destination, disappears irretrievably into the forest. After these first contacts, Fawcett meets the Indigenous people many times – in the movie, he is presented as a gentle but firm man who approaches the locals with understanding and trust. In this movie, there are two crucial moments – the first, when Indigenous people attack a boat, and the second, at the end of the film. In the first case, Fawcett orders his subordinates to stop fighting and start singing, which results in ceasing the attackers to use their bows and attracting their interest in the visitors. They are invited to the village – and that is where an interesting depiction of the life of the Amazon inhabitants appears. The travelers reach a village where elements borrowed from various cultural groups are presented – for example, shrunken human heads are shown for a moment – a practice employed by groups of the western part of the Amazon (while Fawcett traveled in its southern part, through the Brazilian Mato Grosso). The purpose of such a procedure is probably to diversify the image, because in general the Indigenous people are shown without making them more exotic. Fawcett is impressed by some practices, such as stunning fish in water with poison (in the Amazon, many different plants were used for this purpose, depending on the region – Flores 1984: 8); he also allows his face to be painted with red-crushed *achiote* seeds (*Bixa orellana*). The chief of the people is portrayed as a gentle, elderly man who helps the wanderers. In one of the scenes, the entire village is clearly visible – among the houses covered with palm leaves, naked women walk around with children held on their hips (it is noteworthy that intimate body parts are covered with something like "thongs" made of leaves and string, which was not a local practice), baskets, bowls of calabash, clusters of bananas, burning fires, and huge bowls in which some yellow liquid is poured over with a large ladle (rubber? Food for the entire group? Neither reflects the facts). Life is shown as calm and a bit carefree, but certainly not as "savage". Fawcett comments on the presented cornfield with the words "We call them 'savages' while they cultivate the jungle. In a place where no one thought it was possible. We were so arrogant and contemptuous" (Gray 2016, 1:09:21). The presented field is a corn monoculture, which did not take place in terms of Amazonian crops (local gardens were always small and varied in species, which facilitated pest control), but the image of a natural Amazonian garden would probably not impress the viewers.

The movie's final scenes, in which Fawcett meets the locals again, are more controversial, mainly because they are not based on any facts – it is not known what actually happened to the travelers, so it is mainly the director's idea. Fawcett and his son, Jack, come across a group of hostile people in the forest, and the travellers' previous manners of communication fail this time. The travelers flee and encounter a second group of armed natives – there is a struggle between the two groups, and the wanderers are captured. Something like a "judgment" is carried out at the settlement – the shaman, sitting in a circle of warriors opposite the Europeans, states that "the Christian is not one of us", to which the chief replies "He is also not one of them. We must show him the way to the shadows" (Gray 2016, 2:2:16). Up to this point, the Indigenous people are presented in a realistic manner – although not without certain "corrections". However, the following shots raise doubts: Percy and Jack Fawcett are led among metal, carved torches down a fire-lit hill. They drink the liquid given to them by the shaman, lose consciousness, and then are carried into the darkness – and that is how their cinematic fate in the Amazon ends. The entire final ritual looks very stereotypical, refers to elements from Indiana Jones or other popular productions, and differs from the image shown earlier. However, the inhabitants of the village are presented in the film fairly faithfully as Kalapalo from Mato Grosso, who probably had their first full contact with the Western world only in the 1920s (Wilbert 1994: 187). Up to that point, they were mainly engaged in catching fish, as well as growing manioc, corn, beans, and fruit. Kalapalo believe that hunting is an expression of aggression, which is an improper behavior, so for them hunting is not an important way of gaining food (Wilbert 1994: 187). The idea of *ufutisu*, that is, the lack of aggression in public places, is one of the main features of the Kalapalo culture, expressed, among others, by avoiding putting others in an uncomfortable situation as well as by generosity (Basso 2002). Currently, there are more than 400 members of Kalapalo living in eight settlements. The land they once lived in, which still has symbolic and historical significance for them, was partially returned to them, so they can continue to lead a fairly traditional lifestyle and use the old groves planted next to the old settlements (Basso 2002).

Both the movie and the book received positive feedback from critics (e.g., Collin 2017; Dargis 2017) and viewers (although there were also voices regarding the slow narration or return to "monumental cinema" – Bogumilski 2017). Basing the story on a book allowed the director to introduce order to the story, which is historically highly complex – but at the same time, according to John Hemming, a historian of the Amazon, it relieved the creators from completely relying on facts (Hemming 2017). Hemming mainly refuses to recognize Fawcett as an explorer, for example, writing that he was "a geometer who never discovered anything, was a madman, racist, [a person] so incompetent that the only expedition he organized was a five-week disaster" (Hemming 2017). The author also accuses David Grann, the author of the book "The Lost City of Z", of not sticking to the facts and creating an idealistic image of the explorer and a false image of Indigenous groups, and Hollywood following the same lead.

Interestingly, Fawcett's story penetrated into popular culture: in a modern video game, the protagonist finds Fawcett's handkerchief with his initials (PHF – Percival Harrison Fawcett) and a page from his journal in the tropical forest (Crystal Dynamics 2018).

Certain poles of representing the inhabitants of the Amazon – from an image that is fairly faithful on one side to a stereotype one on the other – are present in various texts. Apparently, the Shuar group is one of the most recognizable groups in the Amazon, because apart from comic books or movies in XX century (e.g., Hergé 1937; Gaiman and McKean 1989), it also appeared in XXI century on the TV show "America Express" (TVN 2018), in which people known from the media traveled in pairs through South America with a dollar a day and the items they packed in their backpacks. At the end of the second episode, one of the pairs is rewarded with a day of rest, snapshots of which are later presented to the viewers: the participants spend time in a Shuar settlement, work with them in *chacra* (backyard garden), paint faces using *achiote*, learn how to use a blowgun, etc. There is no commentary behind these images, so the viewers learn nothing about either the ethnic group or its cultural practices. What evokes almost fear among the participants at the end of the first evening of the trip is the *chicha*, which all participants are to try. *Chicha* is a drink popular in the Amazon, prepared from manioc or *platanos* cooked and chewed by women. After such an introduction of saliva enzymes, the resulting mass is set aside for a few days for the fermentation process. Before serving, a little water is added to each portion. People often eat only one meal a day, while they often drink *chicha* – it is very rich in nutrients and perfectly quenches thirst in a hot, equatorial climate. Depending on the group, *chicha* has different names – *tepe* for Huaorani, *asua* for Quichua, or *nijiamanch* for Shuar, etc. This beverage (called *manioc beer* in anthropological literature) plays also a significant role in rituals (see Whitten 1976: 166), as well as expresses the female position in the community (Whitten 1976: 85). Of course, the participants of the "America Express" program do not have the opportunity to learn the value and significance of *chicha* for local residents – they only receive a drink that women in ethnic costumes chew on before their eyes (which in itself is devoid of logic, as *chicha* is not normally chewed before drinking). This task has been described as "disgusting" and "nauseating for the celebrities" (Super Express 2018), so there is no traits of cultural relativism, and the practice has been presented as something degenerated and "abnormal". During the travels of the show's participants around South America, apart from this one episode, they do not go to the Amazon (even though it covers almost one-third of the continent) – they move only along the mountains.

The Kayapó group, which I mentioned earlier, also turns out to be interesting in the eyes of Western culture, because it also found its way to computer games – a Polish production that took over the world of games in 2019 (Creepy Jar 2019) – presents two Indigenous groups: a calm Yabahuaca, which is modeled on Kayapó and Yanomami, as well as a dangerous one, about which we do not learn much. Representatives of the Yabahuaca group, which in the game is visited by an interpreter, have their heads shaved in a manner characteristic for Kayapó, and the chief wears a round, yellow feather bonnet typical for this group, whereas other men have Yanomami hairstyles and long feathers on their forearms, which is also a decoration associated with this group. Representatives of the warrior group who attack the hero during the game have bodies covered with black dye, on which bones are painted in white (in the forest at first glance they look like walking skeletons), and they are modeled probably on the Simbu warriors from Papua New Guinea, who decorated the bodies in this way to scare the opponents (Brown 1995). The protagonist kills all the met Skull Painted Warriors because they constantly attack him. The Yabahuaca are peaceful, but we learn little about them except that they are a "lost tribe", one of 80 of such alive, and their isolation is due to the fear of the outside world. Of course, there are more such groups in the Amazon; however, their isolation results from a conscious decision and rejecting Western culture, rather than from fear. Interestingly, one of the game's protagonists is an anthropologist, and his companion, an interpreter, goes to a Yabahuaca village and calls him for help after more than 30 days – this is where the actual game begins, the main goal of which is to survive in the forest on the way to the village. While on the journey, the protagonist stumbles upon deserted settlements and discovers *ayahuasca* in one of them. He consumes it, leading to a visionary experience where he encounters his partner in the Yabahuaca settlement. During this vision, there is also a glimpse of Indigenous people dancing around a fire in a *shabono*. Therefore, this group is modeled on Yanomami, because their villages are different from all others – they constitute of one large sloping roof over the entire settlement, with a large common area inside. Yanomami do not burn a great fire in the middle as each housewife has her own fire under a roof, but – as I understand it – game portrays the stereotype concerning Indigenous people, who apparently are difficult to be imagined other than dancing around a huge fire. Each village encountered by the protagonist allows him to learn something new to survive (e.g., how to construct a smokehouse, thanks to which it will be easier for him to store food during the travel), so the possibilities of survival also depend on the local skills of people who traditionally inhabit these areas. The Yabahuaca group is described in an interesting manner at the very beginning of the game – in one of the characters' notes we read that "this is their land, their heritage for thousands of years. Anyone who comes here must respect that!" Therefore, cultural relativism is most proper here, and despite cultural distortions in the case of the group called Yabahuaca, the game reflects their cultural practices in a positive way. The situation is slightly different with the Skull Painted Warriors, because we do not learn more about them other than that Yabahuaca are very afraid of them – as it turns out in the course of the game, they constantly attack the main character, that is, the player.

In the notes presented in the game, there is a photo of the Yabahuaca group "from a bird's eye view", and it is almost a faithful reproduction of the most famous photo of the groups remaining out of contact from 2008: three people standing by a palm leaf house and looking up at the flying plane, pointing their weapons at it (Survival International n.d.1) – I understand that the game's protagonists are probably looking for a group similar to this one, which is surprising in itself in view of the policy of not making contact with those who do not want it, which has been promoted for decades (Survival International n.d.1).

In a text posted on an online discussion group, the authors of the game emphasize that they researched information on, for example, how "lost tribes were naturally healing. This applies, for example, to ants' bites on the wound, and then cutting off their bodies, which formed makeshift stitches" (Steam 2018) – of course, these are not the practices of only "lost tribes", because most groups of Amazon Valley used such treatments. In fact, the only explanation for presenting Indigenous people living fully traditionally (that is, like hundreds of years ago) is the concept of "lost tribes" – in the game, contact is to be undertaken with groups which are hardly known and which remain in isolation. The main character is the author of the book about them, but it is the only source of knowledge – this is also where the story includes a mistake, because since an anthropologist wrote a book about Yabahuaca, he should know about this group the most, and thus during the game not be surprised by, for example, visions caused by the *ayahuasca* or the encountered people (a local woman in this vision is wearing a bra and a grass skirt – while seemingly inconspicuous, this element underscores a deficiency in the authors' ability to gather accurate information about Amazonian groups, akin to other shortcomings evident in the game).

Among the culture-based texts depicting the people of the Amazon, the film "Yai Wanonabälewä: The Enemy God" holds a special position (Besette 2008), as it presents a completely different approach. First of all, the creators try to show life from the perspective of the Indigenous people themselves, with their vision of the world, even if it is incomprehensible to the recipient.

"Yai Wanonabälewä" presents the process of Christianization of Yanomami from Venezuela. Determining the genre of this production proves challenging; it strays from a traditional documentary and doesn't strictly adhere to the conventions of a feature film. Rooted in real events and featuring a continuous narrative with a real person portrayed as the main character, it occupies a space on the border between these genres. Nevertheless, in its form, it leans more toward a departure from the documentary film style. The depicted events unfold from the 1950s to the 1990s, with the concluding scenes offering a glimpse into the contemporary situation. The main character is Shake, who in 1950s was a young man chosen by spiritual beings to be a shaman. I will handle the issue of shamanism in the following chapter – here I would like to discuss how Yanomami are presented. In a story, in a way, co-produced by the Indigenous people themselves, we should receive an image as close as possible to the actual state, and, to a large extent, this is the case: in the movie, Yanomami live in a *shabono*, which is an oval community house characteristic for this group, shared by the entire settlement (in the scenes set in the late 20th century and current times, one can already see rectangular houses covered with palm leaves); they use bows and wear characteristic hairstyles and ornaments. However, they constantly have their bodies painted for a ceremony and wear red pieces of fabric on their hips (this is a typical Western representation of Yanomami). The physical elements are only one part of what attracts attention in the film (although, of course, it builds the image of this group) – it is also interesting to present practices that seem – after all – stereotypical.

Yanomami are known for their fierceness – in popular opinion, they are "the most fierce people in the world", and everything they do has its source in the violence that prevails among them. I have already written about this image of Yanomami, because it constitutes an important element in shaping the image of the Amazonian peoples in general. The movie, made in cooperation with Yanomami, does not differ from this image: in every presented issue, violence is emphasized as a permanent element (this applies to both traditional revenge and everyday domestic matters). In his narrative, the protagonist says "We have always been people of revenge" – and this is a real cultural element, because many groups in the region considered a bloody vendetta to be the only possible course of action when something bad happened. However, the movie focuses almost exclusively on how every activity is lined up with violence. This brings the constructed image closer to the stereotype spread by the aforementioned Napoleon Chagnon, an American researcher who in his publications paid particular attention to violence among the Yanomami people. He believed that the permanent state of war in this group affects its social structure and all undertaken actions (Chagnon 1968). Other researchers did not share this opinion – in 2001, Bruce Albert, Alcida Ramos, Kenneth Taylor, and Fiona Watson, anthropologists working with Yanomami wrote: "The four of us spent collectively 80 years working with Yanomami. Each of us speaks one or more Yanomami dialects. Neither of us recognizes the community described in Chagnon's books" (Survival International n.d.2). However, apparently the opinion about "chronic violence" among Yanomami did not miss the filmmakers of "Yai Wanonabälewä", which is all the more interesting because the film is really about shamanism opposed to Christianity and about the process of transitioning from one to the other. Violence is presented as the only context for these events, because it becomes an argument for embracing Christianity, which affirms a human being and thanks to this, the Indigenous people cease fighting among themselves. The proof of the stereotype created by Chagnon in the film may be the name of the group that appears in English-language subtitles (three languages appear in the movie: Indigenous, Spanish, and English in subtitles), because it is written "Yanomamö", and this form was used by the American researcher (others use "Yanomami") – this is a small trace, but it seems significant when compared to the presentation of cultural practices as focused only around violence.

The film was made in 2008, and in 2013, the Yanomami case appeared in the world of anthropology with a new force, because Chagnon published another book – "Noble Savages: My Life Among Two Dangerous Tribes – the Yanomamo and the Anthropologists" (Chagnon 2013) – and in response to it a letter of 18 scientists conducting research with Yanomami appeared, in which they testify that members of this group are generally peaceful and do not agree to "publicly present Yanomami as cruel, violent, archaic people" (Survival International 2013). Such an image is largely present in the film "Yai Wanonabälewä", and although its purpose was – I suspect – to show Indigenous people as Christians rejecting old practices, the image we receive after watching the movie is consistent with Chagnon's vision. This is all the more disturbing, since the film repeatedly emphasizes that it is the real story of the main character, Bautista Cajica from Venezuela, who appears at the beginning of the film, thanking for its production, and, interestingly, his appearance suggests old practices (depicted against a background of a palm leaf wall, with smoke from a fire). In the final scene, he is dressed in a shirt and long pants, wearing glasses. This creates a kind of framework covering the events presented in the movie, although these two narratives are taking place in contemporary times. Perhaps it is a symbolic opening and closing of matters related not only to the life of one person but also to the fate of the entire group.

The opinion about violence among Yanomami is already so widespread that their entire existence is judged from this perspective: for example, one critic wrote that during the movie, the inhabitants of the settlement are "tempted to return to their vengeful ways of life and the entire group risks living in the dark again" (Pluggedin n.d.). From this remark, both the reader and the viewer will receive information, not explicitly articulated, that the life of Indigenous people before Christianization was immersed in "cultural darkness" – they have not yet been provided with the knowledge, "enlightenment" in the form of a religion imposed from above and a new vision of the world.

An intriguing illustration of a reference to the works of Chagnon and his theory, asserting the presence of violence among the Yanomami, is found in a novel by Isabel Allende (2002). According to Chagnon, this violence is linked to the dominance of men characterized by greater courage, as they are perceived as more desirable husbands, thus purportedly having more wives and children (Chagnon and Irons 1979; Chagnon 1988). One of the protagonists of Allende's novel (2002) "La cuidad de las bestias" and participants of an expedition is a researcher who basically represents Chagnon himself – he is a scientist who conducted research among Yanomami, expresses his beliefs about violence and valor, criticizes locals, and emphasizes his important place among anthropologists. He also often refers to his book about Yanomami as a source of knowledge about this group and also emphasizes its widespread popularity not only among students but also among readers not related to the academy. The novel also includes an accusation against Chagnon (Allende 2002: 53), which concerns provoking fights among Indigenous people in order to prove the theory of the importance of warfare in this culture. Chagnon's research was criticized precisely for its ethics (Borofsky 2005: 161–165), and this is reflected in Allende's novel. Other characters, including a local guide, writer, and doctor working with Indigenous groups in the region, repeatedly explain their point of view to the professor and disagree with the unilateral treatment of local people – to some extent, Allende in her book attempts to enter into a discussion with the prevailing Yanomami stereotype. The writer comes from Chile and has been living in Venezuela for years, so she is aware of mistakes made in terms of assessing Indigenous people, and the discussion with the authorities of anthropology and popular opinion seems to be very well implemented. The Indigenous people themselves are presented as a mysterious and determined group, which at the same time is full of "original" wisdom about the world and life. To some extent, Allende has gone over to the side of the "noble savage" who lives in harmony with nature, understanding its order and principles – that is, guided by the knowledge that for us, people from the Euro-American culture, is "magical" and thus incomprehensible. One of the characters even expresses the opinion that Indigenous people "are primitive when it comes to material goods, but they are highly advanced on a mental level" (Allende 2002: 29). Such an opinion also appeared in the stereotype of the "noble savage". Allende also refers to several traditions of Yanomami – talking, for example, about the taboo associated with saying the real name of a given person (Allende 2002: 35; see also Alès 2013: 37), about totem animals (Allende 2002: 44; see also Ogden et al. 2013), as well as about *shabono*. Allende also delves into more intricate issues, including the concept of community, manifested through perspectives that view individualism as a form of madness. Additionally, she explores a nuanced spirituality characterized by animism, wherein the unity of spirit and matter is emphasized (Allende 2002: 44, 33). The author's sympathy for the Indigenous inhabitants of the Amazon is evident through her characters; however, concurrently, she tends to place them in the stereotype of "innocent, wise natives". Allende's work is regarded in terms of the magical realism trend, and this position also exhibits features that allow it to be included in this trend: for example, Indigenous people can disappear and turn into their totem animals. In her novel, Allende even undertakes an "ethnographic" description of culture, but it is rather vague and contains a lot of simplifications, as it is difficult to imagine a "domesticated" boa or jaguar guarding a village or a complete lack of everyday problems. However in Allende's work, Amazonian themes are not extensive; the fact that she has spoken on these matters is significant, as it will undoubtedly have an impact on a wide range of readers.

At a time when Yanomami were "discovered" in the Western world through the works of Chagnon and the subsequent controversies, the story of this group hit the theater – a musical was created about them, in which the narrative was led by Sir David Attenborough, and in a later version by Sting (Rose and Conlon 1983). Thanks to the television version, the topic of destroying the tropical forest and the problems of the Yanomami living there reached a wider audience. In 2010, performative arts returned to the topic in an international project titled "Amazonas. Music Theater in Three Parts" (Weibel 2010). The show not only is the outcome of collaboration among artists from Europe and Brazil but also involves sociologists, anthropologists, and the Yanomami people themselves. Its innovative blend of media art, music theater, technology, and science offers a distinctive perspective on the Amazon's reality (Zentrum für Kunst und Medientechnologie 2010). The titular three parts represent the past, present, and future. In the first part, based on Walter Raleigh's account of his journey to Guyana in 1595 (Raleigh 1595), we get to know the initial contact of one of the Yanomami groups with representatives of Western culture. In this part, the show is carried out as a video installation, and fragments of Raleigh's description are read by actors – this way the expectations of Europeans concerning the resources of the Amazon and its inhabitants are presented (this is a harbinger of later conquest and colonization). In the second part, we discover the problems that exist in the Amazon today, and the elements of this stage of the show are based on a text titled "The Falling Sky" by Davi Kopenawa and Bruce Albert (2013), both mentioned among the project's collaborators. This part presents the Yanomami myth about creating the world and the crack in the sky that appeared due to the undertaking activities in the tropical forest by people from outside – if nothing changes, the "sky will fall" and our world will end. The last part of the show constitutes an awaiting for a solution to the problem of climate change and is presented using the voices of the forest, which acts as one large, living organism, however, not understood by people from outside.

The show is challenging due to its diverse and modern form that combines various techniques and technologies. However, its message is clear and essential: the tropical forest is a unique environment crucial for the world's biological balance. Recognizing this, people should take action to protect and preserve it. Davi Kopenawa was invited to the show's premiere, and he was very satisfied with the results of working on the project and emphasized the importance of undertaking this topic (Kopenawa 2010).

Compared to the seriousness of the previous show, "La Gran Final" (Olivares 2006) constitutes an interesting and somewhat surprising film about Yanomami. The movie presents several Indigenous groups of the world trying to watch the World Cup final in 2002. This is particularly important for Yanomami, as the final match is played between Germany and Brazil. All groups shown in the movie have difficulties with watching the match, mainly due to technical reasons – they have no electricity, equipment, or coverage. However, they all end up watching the game, and the sport brings different groups together – all of them peacefully watch the game together and enjoy the victory of the Brazilian team. I mentioned that this movie is surprising because it contains a completely uncolored, not idealized or exotic image of Yanomami: they are depicted as regular individuals and sports enthusiasts, sprinting through the forest with the desire to catch a glimpse of the game. Their clothes, village, or practices are ordinary, as they are, and even though we do not learn much about the culture itself from this cheerful film, it creates a positive image of the inhabitants of the Amazon.

Yanomami are also known from photos (I deliberately omit all the images placed by tourists on the Internet, because they document their trips – in my analysis, I have taken into account artistic photography exhibitions). The most recognizable artist in this case is Claudia Andujar from Switzerland, who has been living in Brazil for many years. Her photographs capture Yanomami people engaged in everyday activities, yet these images often possess an artistic quality, conveying "something more". Through her works, Andujar actively becomes involved in initiatives advocating for the Yanomami's rights to land and culture (The Guardian 2020). Her photographs not only enhance our understanding of the culture but also play a role in ameliorating the circumstances of the individuals depicted. In 2018, Andujar received the Goethe Medal for her activities, and her works are the flagship representations of Brazil's Indigenous peoples used by organizations acting on their behalf. The Paris exhibition of works by Claudia Andujar in 2020 titled "The Yanomami Struggle" intended to present a cross-section of her photographic works from almost 50 years (Andujar 2020). The exhibition was accompanied by an audiovisual installation titled "Genocide of the Yanomami: Death of Brazil" (Foundation Cartier 2020), which leads the audience from the world of harmony to the world devastated by the culture of the West. A brief introduction to the exhibition was penned by Davi Kopenawa, the renowned representative of the Yanomami, a shaman, and activist. In his message, he expresses

30 Shaping the image of Amazonian Indigenous people

gratitude to Andujar for enlightening him on alternative strategies to combat politicians without resorting to war. He also acknowledges her for showcasing his group members in photographs, recognizing that this exposure will contribute to a broader awareness of their existence (Foundation Cartier 2020). The exhibition included more than 300 photographs presenting not only the life of Yanomami but also – according to the title – their ongoing struggle for the right to cultivate their own culture. Despite the artistic interference in the photographs, we can see much more in these works than just the depiction of people's lives – through the technique of close-ups on the faces or parts of the body, Andujar makes the images universally understandable. In many photographs, the added colors, blurred background, or shifted light (BBC 2020) give the presented people an aura of mystery, not to say exoticism, although Andujar herself admits that she is "connected with the indigenous, with the earth, with the primal struggle. All this deeply touches me" (Foundation Cartier 2020), so her works do not aim to exoticize the subject, but rather to present it in a manner that resonates with the viewer, provoking reflection on the conveyed message.

An interesting example of an installation concerning Yanomami and their mythology is the project "The Cosmic Anaconda" (Slovenski Etnografski Muzej 2011a), which consists of 201 baskets made by Yanomami. The handicraft, arranged along walls representing a giant snake, winds through the exhibition room, accompanied by the sounds of traditional songs performed by women. The installation represents the "indigenous spirit of ancient knowledge" (Slovenski Etnografski Muzej 2011b), and although the Indigenous people are not physically depicted, they are present both in visual, sound, and ideological communication – their traditional knowledge, which pertains to the balance of the world, is posited to be the solution to the challenges faced by the modern world.

Artistic projects centered around the Yanomami were also showcased by Barbara Navarro, a French artist who frequently journeys to the Amazon. The inhabitants of *shabono* in photographs are presented in various contexts, mainly when painting their bodies with red dye from *Bixa orellana*, as well as during everyday activities (Navarro 2018); however, the image that emerges from these representations is mainly related to the time before contact. Another project by Navarro is similar and consists of two children's books (Navarro 2014a, 2015) and a related movie. In the books, the author presented the daily life of Yanomami – stories about a girl named Meromi and a boy named Namowë constitute a pretext to show various cultural practices, as well as myths (e.g., Meromi discovers her destiny to become a shaman and therefore – according to Yanomami myths – she has the ability to transform into different animals). A short documentary accompanying the books (Navarro 2014b) presents the village of Yanomami and daily works, such as fishing, returning from hunting, preparing food, decorating the body, as well as shamanistic practices. The shots (presented without additional commentary) are intertwined with illustrations from Navarro's books. Representatives of this group are presented realistically, and simply, the role of the family, common security, and living in harmony is emphasized, but the image is maintained – as I mentioned – in the "before contact" convention, that is, Yanomami are shown as if they live in the same manner as more than 60 years ago. In Barbara Navarro's works, there are almost no war issues with Yanomami, because – let us emphasize once again – this is not the basic characteristic of this group.

Yanomami without any aspects of violence are also presented in comic book by Milo Manara (2008). The Italian cartoonist, known mostly for erotic comic books, diverged from his usual subject matter in this text. He delved into a different theme – a satire on mass culture. The main character, Bergman, after taking up the challenge of adventure gets lost in the tropical forest and ends up in a local "hospitable settlement" (Manara 2008: 47). The local people wear loincloths (the author did not draw any underwear, which often happens in other cases); their ears are adorned with ornaments crafted from feathers and sticks. In the background and in the bird's eye view, it is possible to see a communal house of Yanomami. Bergman is invited to the chief, who turns out to be a shaman, because he gives him *yopo* (otherwise known as *yãkõana*, a hallucinogenic powder prepared from the bark of trees of the genus *Virola* – PIB n.d.). The protagonist enters a trance, during which he watches various scenes of violence. One of the locals comments about a "sad state of consciousness" (Manara 2008: 52). The shaman presented in the story is a balding old man possessing not only knowledge of the supernatural world but also a narrative one – it turns out that he is at the service of the organizer of the Bergman's adventure. Interestingly, there is no baldness among Amazonian people, but it is a trifle compared to the general image of Yanomami in this comic book: they not only are not shown as being guided by violence (later they do shoot at Bergman with bows, but they do it at the command of a shaman who orders them not to hit the target, which they perform perfectly) but also as fused with nature – at the end of the protagonist's adventure, the shaman symbolically turns into a tree, and the entire village disappears in the forest. In one of his statements, the shaman says that in the "real" world, Indigenous people do not really exist (Manara 2008: 61) – we do not learn whether this is an objective remark or a foresight for the future, but it does not sound optimistic. Later during his adventures, Bergman meets another Yanomami who sits on a tree on a flooded terrain and remains silent throughout the scene. Bergman, in his monologue, expects death at the hands of the native, which ultimately happens despite the main character's assurances that he respects the inhabitants of the forest (Manara 2008: 97; at this point, the quite absurd adventure turns into a grotesque one, in which the protagonist's cut off head still takes part in the events, so that in the end it turns out that there is no line between what is true and what is not).

A similar technique of blurring the line between the real and the imaginary was used by James Rollins in his novel (2002), but here it leads to a different solution – his characters meet with the inhabitants of the Amazon represented by the Yanomami and then end up with the Ban-ali, who originated with the Yanomami, but had profoundly changed. The novel turns out to be a thriller, although not from the very beginning. The story is based on a well-known plot scheme of an unexplained event: four years earlier, a group of researchers disappeared, from which unexpectedly one man returns in a near death condition – an unusual element is that when he set off on the journey he had only one arm, but returns with both. This fact intrigued not only the local population or the missionary, whom the dying traveler reached, but also the army. A journey into the forest is undertaken to find an Indigenous group that marked the deceased with a tattoo which scares the local population. In the novel, a description of this group appears at the beginning: "tribe that mates with jaguars and whose members can vanish into thin air. They bring death to all who encounter them", and they are commonly called the Blood Jaguars (Rollins 2002: 63). The initial description of the inhabitants of the Amazon is not any more optimistic, but concerns Yanomami, whose name the author translates as "violent people", and "its members were considered ruthless warriors. . . . They were known to wipe out an entire village for so slight an insult as calling someone a derogatory name" (Rollins 2002: 29). We also learn that "the Yanomami were superb hunters skilled with bow, blowgun, spear, and club" (Rollins 2002: 29). Some of the characters know the representatives of the local residents well, but it is their thoughts and statements that the above quotations come from. This brings the reader dangerously close to the popular opinion about Yanomami as ruthless warriors – an opinion that anthropology has been trying to fight for 50 years. However, it is not Yanomami who are the main characters of the book, but the aforementioned Ban-ali. When, after a long and unusual journey, the characters reach them, the people are shown as ordinary inhabitants of these areas from old times – dressed only in a loincloth, they have bodies painted in black (probably with dye from *Genipa americana* seeds commonly used in the Amazon), and live in huts, which, however, are quite unusually built on trees. The valley is defined by the presence of a towering tree that stands out among all others in the vicinity. We soon receive more remarkable information: "countless generations ago, most likely during the first migration of people into South America, the tribe must have stumbled upon the tree's remarkable healing ability and became enthralled by it. Becoming *ban-yin* – slaves" (Rollins 2002: 356), which led to such profound genetic changes that "Ban-ali were near to leaving *Homo sapiens* behind, becoming their own species" (Rollins 2002: 359). This is due to the remarkable symbiosis between the tree and local inhabitants – it offers them health benefits exclusively within the confines of the valley where the tree resides. The Ban-ali also have an advantage over other groups of the region, because the tree provides them with a unique sense of organization and ingenuity (Rollins 2002: 377). Thus, the author of the novel indirectly implies that without "miraculous help" the Indigenous people would not be able to conduct proper logistics and create inventions – after all, the author unambiguously presented them at the beginning of the book as warriors with a low level of reflection: the Ban-ali group is Yanomami only as if "healed" – in an unspoken idea probably "healed from savagery".

The novel also includes information about another group from the Amazon region – Shuar from Ecuador. One of the protagonists comes from this group, and her image is clearly negative – she cannot speak, is "threateningly silent", and kills with a certain amount of satisfaction. From the first moment she appears in the course of events, we learn that for Shuar these are "normal" behaviors, among which "infidelity and murder were common" (Rollins 2002: 74) as well as rape (Rollins 2002: 454). The author did not fail to twice mention *tsantsas*, that is, shrunken heads, for which this group was formerly known (Rollins 2002: 74, 399), but in both cases this information is provided in the context of sensationality, which only perpetuates the stereotypes about the Shuar people. In general, this is how Indigenous people are presented in Rollins' novel – although two western characters have been living in Indigenous villages for years, and the third even comes from the local people (but he is a scientist, a respected professor, which probably justifies his presence in the group of travelers of Western origin), we receive an image of the natives living in the Amazon in a very simplified version. They are not full-fledged characters but only constitute a background for events experienced by Americans – despite the fact that some of the events are arranged by the local people themselves in order to defend their territory. As it is not difficult to guess, Americans (represented in two groups, i.e., scientific and troublemakers) destroy the valley inhabited by Ban-ali and do not allow them to continue living in their traditional way (of course, as it happens in such stories, they do it in the "best interest" of the local people themselves, which in itself shows the arrogance of characters).

A similar role of supporting characters for the events of the members of the two groups, scientific and gangster, is played by Indigenous people in Nick Thacker's crime novel (Thacker 2016) – they turn out to make a bloody sacrifice using the captured representatives of the West, and their leader is presented as a merciless murderer. In the course of the novel, the characters end up in a village made of stone blocks and tree trunks, and the scientists observe that "the natives, to the outside observer, were generally considered quite primitive, but ... there were balance of power between the jungle itself and its inhabitants" (Thacker 2016: 254). Therefore, the author presents the Indigenous in two ways – first as valiant and cruel, and later as almost idyllic, representing the stereotype of the inhabitants of Eden. Ann Patchett (2011) uses a similar mechanism in her novel about doctors trying to create a new drug from the bark of a tree used by Indigenous people of the Brazilian tropical forest. The novel presents two local groups, both isolated until recently, but a researcher of exotic mushrooms managed to reach only the first group (the character, which is shown only in the stories of other characters, resembles

Richard Evans Schultes, a well-known botanist who traveled in the Amazon at the beginning of the 20th century). Researchers work with members of the group among which they live – over time we learn that local residents are not interested in the research carried out by the newcomers, but they passively submit to them, allowing them to take samples of blood or other body fluids. This community possesses a unique and remarkable trait – women maintain their fertility until old age. This results in a high number of children in the village, with many families spanning up to five generations (Patchett 2011: 79). An American company finances research that would enable the production of drug supporting fertility even after menopause – the reason for the events turns out to be the bark of one species of trees growing near the village. The inhabitants are shown to be quite impassive and as a submissive group of people that the researchers call "primitive" (Patchett 2011: 82). There is no deeper description of cultural practices in the novel – the local people are only a pretext to show the behaviors and "discoveries" of the newcomers from Western culture. During the presented events, there is also a second group of Indigenous people, who refuse to make contact. Stereotypically, it's a group of cannibals spreading terror, killing anyone who gets close to their territory. So once again, we are dealing with two stereotypical examples: one idyllic, the other valiant.

The novel includes one more topic worth noting: the main doctor conducting research in the settlement is shown as keeping Indigenous people in fear – they perform work for her and allow themselves to be examined out of fear, not out of conviction (Patchett 2011: 262, 271). As she says herself, she "tamed them" (Patchett 2011: 214) over several decades of work – but at that time, she did not learn the language, she still did not understand their customs, and she carried out all the tests without their consent (Patchett 2011: 194). It resembles a real person from several decades ago who treated the locals similarly, although in the name of another idea – Rachel Saint working with the Huaorani group in Ecuador. The missionary, who initially worked with the Summer Institute of Linguistics (SIL), after contacting the Huaorani groups, organized their transfer to one place where she had control over them. Although she learned the Huao terero language, she worked on converting Huaorani to the Christian faith. After removing SIL from Ecuador in 1981 (Goffin 1994: 93), Rachel Saint secured funding in the United States, allowing her to stay with the Huaorani people until her passing in 1995 (Ziegler-Otero 2007). The effects of her work are assessed in various ways, but most often negatively – bringing individual groups into one place led to excessive use of forest resources, the spread of diseases, hunger, as well as changes in the social structure (Wierucka 2015: 60). Similar missionary endeavors occurred, and in Patchett's novel, the doctor similarly neglects the cultural practices of the local inhabitants in pursuit of an idea entirely foreign to the natives.

The aforementioned topic of the process of converting Huaorani and missionary work constitutes the main theme of the movie "End of the Spear"

(Hanon 2005). In its structure, this production draws inspiration from a documentary, as the narrative is guided by a character portrayed as a young boy. This approach fosters a complete acceptance of the presented information. Right from the opening scene, it is declared that the story is rooted in real events, establishing the lens through which the movie is to be perceived.

The presented story refers to the events of 1956 and 1958 in Ecuador, where contact was made with the Huaorani group. Until 1956, members of this group remained out of contact with the Ecuadorian nation, and there were several reasons for this: the Huao terero language they speak is an isolated language, with no elements in common with any other language; they were known at that time mainly for their courage in defending their territory, as well as for the battles between individual groups. The movie shows the search for the Huaorani settlement by American pilots but omits the fact that the pilots were missionaries whose goal was to convert Huaorani to the Christian faith. The reason for the presented search is the economic development of Ecuador and plans to send the army to look for Indigenous settlements (Hanon 2005, 00:19:03), which is not entirely true (in fact, the main goal was to convert Huaorani to Christianity and open their lands to the development of the oil industry). The same applies to the Huaorani war traditions portrayed in the movie as another justification for the necessity of contact – while these traditions did exist, their extent might not have been accurately depicted (scenes of slaughter are shown several times, and warriors are presented as soulless killing machines). Already in the first sentences of the narrative, we learn that more than half of the group died as a result of fratricidal battles and this led them to the "edge of extinction" (Hanon 2005, 00:2:52), which again is not true. The theme of the fights also refers to the figure of Moipa, known in this group for his particular bravery and violence, but the character we see in the film should not appear in it, because he lived more than 20 years earlier, in the 1930s (Wierucka 2015: 105–106)[1] and not in 1956 – he was undeniably portrayed among the warriors to highlight the perceived exceptional cruelty of the Huaorani, against which the missionaries had to advocate for peaceful engagement. There is no need to underscore the inaccuracy of this portrayal.

The Huaorani culture is also not presented honestly: starting with their clothes that, in a "Christian" manner, cover the intimate parts of the body (Huaorani traditionally wore only *come*, a string tied on their hips), to the *macho* lifestyle in which a man kidnaps a woman from another village to "make him a drink" as a wife (Hanon 2005, 26:53) – however in Huaorani culture, there existed (and to a significant extent still exists) a form of egalitarianism, wherein women are not subjected to men, in contrast to the hierarchical relationships found in many other cultures. In the movie, women are completely dependent on men, they are beaten by them and beg for mercy – it is something unthinkable in the Huaorani group. In the movie, the group is led by a commander deciding about the fate of all its members, and Huaorani did not have such a position (mainly due to the above-mentioned egalitarianism) – some could be more respected due to their age or experience, but this did not entitle them to have power over others (Yost 1981: 109).

The film has an unequivocal tone: the Huaorani would have slaughtered each other if they had not been helped by missionaries whose faith forbids killing. The Indigenous are portrayed as people guided by lies and extreme emotions and are completely irrational. Undoubtedly, for the world associated with missionary work, this type of people is needed to justify the conversion to Christianity.

The plot of "End of the Spear" brings together two stories – the tragic death of missionaries in 1956 (the scene of their death is shown using long, slow shots, emphasizing their martyrdom) and the contact carried out in 1958 by women associated with the missionaries (namely the sister and wife of two of them). In the latter case, the protagonists provide medical assistance; they are interested in the Huaorani world; and we do not learn about their negative impact on local residents by working with the Summer Institute of Linguistic described above and the changes introduced to everyday practices, as well as opening up the areas traditionally owned by Huaorani to oil companies (Wierucka 2015: 59).

Issues related to these events continued, both in art and life. Here, it is worth noting the documentary film "Beyond the Gates of Splendor" (Hanon 2004), which was made before the feature film and was based on a book written by the widow of one of the missionaries (Elliot 1957). The document emphasizes the martyrdom of five missionaries, the sacrifice made by their wives, and the role of forgiveness – after years, the son of a killed missionary is friends and lives with his father's killer. The message of the document is clearly missionary, which is not surprising due to the case of the martyrdom of five pilots still recalled in the United States.

A similar message is expressed by a second documentary made by the same director (Hanon 2007), who tells the story of the grandson of one of the missionaries killed by Huaorani – the entire trilogy is called "Walk His Trail Trilogy", which "tells the unforgettable and inspiring story of killing five missionaries by a stone age tribe [living] deep in the Amazon jungle" (NewsWire 2011). The missionary nature of the trilogy is emphasized in every part – in the feature film Nate Saint, one of the missionaries, becomes a saint in Huaorani's account while still alive (in the sky, there is an "extraordinary" light in which you can see celestial beings calling the wounded missionary to themselves), and similar images are also cited in both documents. None of these films presents the objective (or at least partially objective) truth about the events due to the purpose of their production: justifying the process of converting Indigenous peoples to Christianity and emphasizing the martyr death of the missionaries.

All three films – feature and two documentaries – were well received by the audience and critics (one of the documentaries received two film awards[2]) and thus consolidated the image of Huaorani as ruthless warriors. Such an opinion is quite common (Wierucka 2015: 129–135). Another feature that is supposed to reflect the "true" character of Huaorani is their "living in harmony with nature" – this can be seen especially in photo exhibitions. One of the most famous photographs come from the exhibition titled "Before they pass away" by Jimmy Nelson (Nelson n.d.) – to carry out this project, the artist visited many Indigenous groups from all over the world, including Huaorani. They are depicted in beautiful, color dimmed shots, some with a slightly smoky light adding some mystery to the scenes – and they are shown as before 1956, that is, completely without the influence of Western culture: they walk naked (although the intimate parts of the body are covered with leaves wrapped around the traditional *come*), they have faces painted with *achiote* (*Bixa orrellana* is used by Huaorani during holidays – however, Nelson's photos show that they use it every day, which certainly adds exoticism), they do not use any plastic or metal equipment (and in every settlement they are commonly used), etc. Nelson captures an image expected by the audience – Indigenous people, who are supposed to look like "Indians". I wonder how the photographer talked to the locals – did he ask them for "ethnic look" . . .? The photos are undoubtedly beautiful, and perhaps as a work of art, they reflect some truth about Huaorani, but I do not think that it is even partially objective. A similar image is captured in photographs by Pete Oxford, in which Huaorani as "forest people" live as they did 60 or more years ago (Oxford n.d.). In one of them, an Indigenous woman even carries water in a clay jug, and the caption for the photo says "a unique shape of clay vessels made by Huaorani compared to other groups of Ecuador", while the shape of the jug held by the woman resembles those made by Quichua. The general description of the photos also includes information about "the traditional hostility of Huaorani and killing many people who wanted to enter their territory" (Oxford n.d.), which emphasizes the negative stereotype about this group. Pete Oxford's photos were included in his album titled "The Spirit of the Huaorani" (Oxford and Bish 2009), whose cover presents a photo of a man with a spear running through the forest – his stance expresses tension and focus, and the hunter himself is probably just a moment before attacking. This dynamic image in a way contrasts with the description on the back of the cover that the author attempts to "reveal to the whole world the warm, gentle, and humorous character of Huaorani" (Oxford and Bish 2009, cover). As it can be seen, it is not difficult to go from one extreme to another. Oxford also took beautiful and stylized photos of other Amazon groups – Machiguenga, Yaminahua, or Campa (Oxford n.d.).

Huaorani were also portrayed in the photos of a Hungarian artist, Attila Loránt. In his 2007 album "Wapponi" (Lorant 2007), he included partially stylized pictures of the people during their daily work. Loránt is the founder of the "Disappearing Cultures" foundation, and within it he presents various cultural groups of the world – the manner of presenting them probably intends to emphasize what is "disappearing", and therefore the photos are stylized to look like everyday life before contact with the Western world (if there was no such contact, they would probably not be "disappearing"). The title of the album refers to the word *huapponi*, most often heard in Huaorani groups, meaning, depending on the context, among others, "well, all right, well enough", which reflects the nature of the presented photos. Lóránt also photographed other groups of the region, including Enawene Nawe and Kamayura from Brazil, whom he presented similarly to the Huaorani. They were included in the album "Indiánok" (Lóránt 2006).

A different example of representing Indigenous people of the Amazon can be found in a novel by Mario Vargas Llosa titled "El sueño del celta" ("The Dream of the Celt", Llosa 2012 [2010]), in which the author presents the story of Roger Casement, a British diplomat and at the same time an Irish nationalist. Casement, a real person living at the turn of the 19th and 20th centuries, is full of contradictions and controversies – and although it is fascinating in itself, I am interested in the manner in which the Amazonian Indigenous people are portrayed in the novel. Vargas Llosa, in his earlier 1987 novel "The Storyteller" (Llosa 1989), dealt with this topic by presenting the special role of storytellers in the Machiguenga group from Peru. The Peruvian writer is known for his involvement in social, cultural, and political affairs, not only in fiction but also in the factual literature and personal activities (Greenberg 2018). In many texts, he dealt with the affairs of people oppressed and deprived of rights, believing in the power of individual morality and the will to change (Greenberg 2018). The novel "The Dream of the Celt" was the writer's first work after receiving the Nobel Prize (Nobel Prize 2010), and it dealt with, among others, the Indigenous cultures of the Amazon. In "The Dream of the Celt", this is directly related with the main character, as Roger Casement was sent by the British government to investigate allegations of abuse in the Putumayo River area (at the beginning of the 20th century in Peru, currently in Colombia). The UK-based Peruvian Amazon Company (PAC) producing and selling rubber, headed by Julio César Arana, was active in Putumayo, called in short Casa Arana. As in any similar case during the *rubber boom*, the employees of the company were locals, who not only were forced to work against their will but also were severely punished when not reached the quota – they were whipped, marked with the Casa Arana brand, their hands, feet, or ears were cut off, they were tortured in various ways, and if it failed, the same actions were applied to members of their families, that is, wives and children. Reports of these practices have reached Europe and the British Government has ordered Roger Casement to closely examine the matter. The diplomat was already known for similar actions: in 1903, he prepared a report revealing numerous abuses of the rubber industry in the Congo (Louis 1964: 99), which was then ruled by the Belgian king Leopold II. Casement became known as a defender of the rights of Indigenous peoples, and his report had a great impact on both changing the policy and the situation in the Congo itself (Louis 1964). The diplomat traveled to the Amazon together with a special commission, and then, after returning in 1912, he published a report describing what he encountered in the Putumayo region. Casement himself was shocked by what he saw – in a vast area controlled by Arana's company, local people were forced to work beyond human power. Slave labor led to exhaustion, disease, hunger, and the death of thousands of people. Casement's expedition resulted in his so-called Blue Book (Casement 1912).[3] The report resulted in a judicial process of the owners of the PAC and, over time, completely terminating this company.

Putumayo is still inhabited by Indigenous groups belonging to three language families: witoto (Witoto, Ocaina, and Nanuya languages), bora (Bora, Miraña, and Muinane languages), and Andoke (an isolated language) (Wilbert 1994: 364). All these groups exhibit some cultural similarities in terms of their livelihoods: they grow gardens (mainly manioc, bananas, *platanos*, papayas, pineapples, sweet potatoes, mangoes, etc.), hunt different species of animals, and also fish. The focal point of social life revolves around a communal home, and the primary principle of social organization is a patrilineal system of kinship (Wilbert 1994: 365). Everyday life is closely related to rituals that regulate the relationship between people and the natural environment. At the beginning of the 20th century, there were about 50,000 representatives of various Witoto groups, but by 1930, only one-tenth remained due to the Peruvian Amazon Company's activity in the area (Echeverri 2010: 49).

In Llosa's book, Casement is portrayed as a defender of the rights of Indigenous peoples, a righteous but erring man. Casement's encounters with Indigenous people presented in the novel are shocking from the very beginning – at the first instance, local residents are shown as a group awaiting punishment for providing insufficient amount of rubber. After a moment, they are burned alive as a "lesson" for the remaining slaves (Llosa 2012: 150). PAC employees, with whom the diplomat talks, call the Indigenous people "savages", "cannibals", and murderers of their own children (Llosa 2012: 179), who pay tribute to the anaconda (Llosa 2012: 198). In Llosa's narrative, Casement concludes that for all these people, the Indigenous "were not, strictly speaking, human beings, but inferior, contemptible form of existence" (Llosa 2012: 181). The author focuses more on the fate and dilemmas of the Irishman than on depicting the local inhabitants of the Amazon, because the central theme of the novel is the figure of a diplomat whom Llosa at some point calls, through the mouth of Joseph Conrad, the "British Bartolomé de las Casas" (Llosa 2012: 59). This also proves the author's attitude toward the main character of his novel. In turn, the Indigenous people are shown as gentle, easily subordinate people who cannot fight the overwhelming power of the invaders, which gives the main character an impulse to think about the fate of his own nation – he states that the fight should be now, immediately, before the Irish become as submissive and helpless as the Indigenous people, due to the violence of the English. He also comes to the conclusion that regardless of the location, "the same horrors were repeated, with minor variations, inspired by greed, the original sin that accompanied human beings from birth, the hidden inspiration of their infinite wickedness" (Llosa 2012: 151). Despite presenting problems related to the *rubber boom* in the novel, Llosa did not include a clear image of Indigenous people. Similar to Casement's report in his "Blue Book", Llosa uses local people's characters to expose the activities of the rubber baron and his subordinates. One of the few descriptions of local residents concerns the Yagua group, when the main character of the novel mentions a meeting with them and the impressions made on him by plant fiber skirts (Llosa 2012: 250). In addition, the book includes the names of Witoto, Ocaina, Muinane, Nonuya, Andoke, Rezígaro, and Bora, but without detailed descriptions. Therefore, Llosa's work does not reveal a specific image of the Amazonian Indigenous peoples but presents their fate at the beginning of the 20th century, when the collection of rubber was the main driving force behind the activities of both local and foreign entrepreneurs.

Report by Casement and the novel version of the latter's life do not constitute a deeper reflection on the Indigenous side of the conflict related to collecting rubber, while, as Juan Alvaro Echeverri writes, matters related to those times are unresolved for the local residents (Echeverri 2010: 50). He discusses the inaugural journey of the descendants of individuals who perished at the hands of PAC torturers to the site of their ancestors' demise, marking the first such expedition since the early 20th century. Old men had to face their dramatic post-memory in order to be able to regain the territory that is related to their ritual life and the social organization – they had to "regain a thread of their life" (Echeverri 2010: 51). The main headquarters building of the PAC is still standing (despite Casement's dreams expressed in the novel that everything will soon be devoured by the forest and there will be no trace of the rubber baron's activity – Llosa 2012: 322) and is a reminder of those events for the Indigenous people. However, the main purpose of returning to this place and time is reconstructing society, for which historical awareness and new common memory are necessary (Echeverri 2010: 55). From the point of view of the Indigenous inhabitants of the Putumayo region, the *rubber boom* constituted not only exploitation and slave labor bringing death to entire groups – it also stood for the destruction of cultural practices, deprivation of rituals, and tearing apart social tissue, which cannot be completely repaired. According to the way of thinking of local residents, these experiences should be used to build the future, not to close oneself in the past (Echeverri 2010: 60). It is also interesting that in the Amazon the name of Casement is still known and respected – he is rightly considered a hero who, despite everything, tried to reveal the truth and demanded justice (Pollak 2016).

In turn, the movie "El Abrazo de la Sierpente" (Guerra 2015) presents groups that no longer exist in the Amazon and also depicts historical figures visiting the area – it is based on the diaries of two people: Theodore Koch-Grünberg from the early 20th century and Richard Evans Schultes from the 1940s. Therefore, the stories are set nearly 50 years apart, and even though the events are based on some facts, as the director emphasizes, they are fictional (ScreenPrism n.d.). The movie presents the journey of two researchers across the Amazon accompanied by the same guide, the last representative of his group. Researchers are looking for the *yakruna* plant, which is sacred to the local inhabitants due to its healing properties, and – what is valuable for the Western world – it helps in the processing of rubber tree juice. Both explorers, despite the time difference, are led by the same guide, Karamakate, and in fact he is the actual protagonist, not the travelers. We meet him as a young man who is convinced that his entire group was killed in the course of fighting, so he lives alone. Other groups call Karamakate "the world mover" which probably refers to his shamanistic practices, but it is not ultimately explained in the film. The young Karamakate becomes the only guide of the seriously ill Grünberg. The researcher informs the shaman that his people, referred to as Cohiuano in the movie, still inhabit a distant village. They decide to journey there together, as the elusive *yakruna* also thrives in that location. After reaching the settlement, Karamakate discovers that his group has succumbed to alcoholism and other bad influences of Western culture and has lost the traditions developed over the centuries. At this point, the shaman once again becomes the only representative of his culture, because everyone else lost it. It is arguably one of the most poignant moments in the movie when Karamakate enters the village and witnesses cultural decay, a profound lack of understanding, lack of respect for everything that was sanctified by the old way of life. He also finds *yakruna* there and destroys it, because he believes that no one is worthy of it anymore – neither locals nor strangers. At the end of the film, 50 years later the second researcher, Schultes, travels with Karamakate and the latter shows the traveler the last *yakruna* plant, which grows high in the mountains – and gives it to Schultes, stating that his own destiny was not to pass knowledge on to his people, but to the researcher. Earlier in the movie, Grünberg's helper says that "if the 'whites' do not learn [Indigenous knowledge], it will be our [Indigenous] end" (Guerra 2015, 1:31:02) – how dramatic it sounds especially in the light of many contemporary events disregarding traditional knowledge.

Karamakate is reluctant to cooperate with Europeans from the very beginning, but in the case of Grünberg, he is persuaded by the researcher's assistant, and 50 years later – an illustration sketched by Schultes in his notebook, because it is a vision from a dream that – as it turns out – the shaman and Schultes share. In many groups of the Amazon, dreams are treated as an indicator of important events – for example, among Ese Eja from Peru and Bolivia, sleep visions define the names of children, as well as everyday activities, such as hunting or gardening. Animals appearing in a dream are assigned meanings and resulting actions (e.g., a hawk foreshadows contact with a jaguar, a collared peccary – a good day to catch fish, etc. – Peluso 2004: 107–119). For Huaorani from eastern Ecuador, the content of dreams is also read as a certain divination and interpreted by a shaman (e.g., the dream of a harpy – *Harpia harpyja* – foreshadows that hunters will find a large herd of peccary, and a dream of crossing a river and not being able to reach the other bank means an upcoming disease – Wierucka 2015: 166). The significance of dreams is emphasized in the film, because Karamakate goes with the researcher on a journey only due to a shared dream, and he discovers the dream's meaning at the very end of the journey: he is to pass his knowledge to the researcher.

During the journey with the shaman, both researchers go to the same places, including a mission area. At the beginning of the 20th century, it is shown as a place of eradication of culture among Indigenous children: the mission prohibits using local languages and names, but it also does not cultivate and use local knowledge, which is necessary for long-term survival (e.g., the habit of not eating fish before the rainy season[4]). The mission area also includes a small monument from 1907 erected to "recognize the courage of Colombian rubber pioneers who brought civilization to the land of savages-cannibals and showed them the way to God and his holy church" (Guerra 2015, 1:00:10). After reading this inscription, young Karamakate meets with the boys working in the kitchen, speaks to them in their language and teaches them the myth of a gift that the ancestors received from the gods. Probably the same boys, now adults, meet Schultes and Karamakate 50 years later – they are fanatical followers of a self-proclaimed prophet who recognizes himself as the son of God. The madness of events on the mission is real, because such events took place in this area (McCullough n/a). The shaman in the movie comments that these people have become the worst in both worlds (Guerra 2015, 1:18:05) – because they are no longer culturally Indigenous, but lost in the religious teachings introduced by the missions they cannot find themselves in any of the worlds. The film also refers to the *rubber boom*, exploitation related to the collection of rubber – in a scene from the beginning of the 20th century, a crippled local man expects torture and death because he did not provide enough rubber tree juice. Memories of working for the so-called rubber baron also torment the Indigenous person accompanying Grünberg.

The move constitutes not only an image of the impact of colonization on local groups, but it also attempts to present these events from the side of local residents. The values represented by Karamakate are in decline, because other representatives of local groups no longer respect them – the clash of his vision of the world with what he finds in the settlements is painful, all the more so because he is the only one perceiving it. Interestingly, the actor playing the role of the older Karamakate, Antonio Bolívar, was himself one of the last representatives of Ocaina culture[5] (in 2005, the group consisted of 285 people living in Colombia and Peru – Ministerio de Cultura 2019) and many representatives of other local groups participated in producing the film, including Witoto, Tikuna, Cubeo, Yurutí, Tukano, Siriano, Karapano, and Desano (McCullough n/a). In the movie, it is stated several times that the characters from Europe do not understand anything, because they are "white" – at this point, it is not about the color of the skin but about a certain philosophy of life and way of perceiving the world. The shaman orders the travelers to get rid of all belongings, because in his opinion they prevent them from truly opening up to a different perception of the reality surrounding them. As a result, we understand that what we are seeing is a commentary on the present: our world has not been able to open up to other modes of thinking for five centuries, and the only result of colonization is a change in the thinking of the Indigenous inhabitants of the Amazon, which leads to a cultural and ecological catastrophe. Karamakate comments, "All your science leads only to violence and death" (Guerra 2015, 00:49:42) which again becomes painfully true when we look at the history of the Amazon and other areas occupied by representatives of the Western culture.

Returning to the image of the Indigenous inhabitants of the Amazon in this production, it is difficult not to admit its uniqueness: many cultural aspects were portrayed by Indigenous people themselves, and although the presented culture is fictional, it contains elements supported by both the ethnographic description of two researchers whose journals were used and the knowledge of the locals themselves. In contrast to other films, the Indigenous characters are depicted as calm, balanced, and proud of their customs. Their demeanor undergoes a transformation only following contact with Western culture when they lose their values and traditional knowledge. Therefore, the movie not only pays tribute to local cultures but also presents a poignant critique of the colonization process and its associated degenerations.

The film received great reviews from critics (e.g., Stein 2016; Kermode 2016) and was also nominated for the Film Academy Award as the best non-English-language film of 2016 and won many awards (including at the Cannes Festival).

Charmian Hussey in her novel "The Valley of Secrets" (2005) also refers to the journey of Schultes, as well as three botanists from the turn of the 19th and 20th centuries, that is, the previously described Henry Bates, Alfred Wallace, and Richard Spruce. The main character discovers the Amazon from the beginning of the 20th century through the travel journals of his grandfather's brother, so the reader learns about the reality from over a hundred years ago, but the reactions of travelers and their experiences are not typical for that period. Extensive fragments of the journals included in the novel show the sensitivity and lack of prejudice of young heroes undertaking a more than a year-long expedition into the Amazon forest: contrary to Western practices at that time, they become friends with Indigenous people and live with them in the settlement, and over time they become members of the group. Thanks to this closeness, the reader is presented with the world of everyday life of local people, their work, as well as – as it turns out in the later part of the book – problems with enslavement, kidnappings, and all the dramatic events related to the *rubber boom*.

The group described by Hussey is not clearly defined, but some features are quite distinctive: the people wear colored feathers in their earlobes, have long hair, use bows to hunt, and grow gardens. The bibliography provided at the end of the novel (this is an unusual and interesting element of the book) includes well-known titles concerning the Yanomami (Hanbury-Tenison 1982) or Wayapí groups (Campbell 1995), so it can be presumed that the fictional name Taluma hides elements of various cultures of the region. The author of the novel tries to tell how different the approach of people from Western culture would be if they took the trouble to get to know the Indigenous people, and not just treat them as a workforce – the travelers at the beginning of the 20th century meet their later friends as "savages", but in the course of events they turn out to be extraordinary, helpful, and friendly people – of course, it is also the result of the openness of the characters. The description in the journal presents Indigenous as living in harmony with each other and with nature, gentle (Hussey 2005: 268), possessing great knowledge of the tropical forest (Hussey 2005: 346), accepting the world around them, and deprived of the "need for possessions or for power" (Hussey 2005: 346). From this idealized image, the author goes on to reflect (through her young character) that if all people were like this, everyone would be able to live in harmony (Hussey 2005: 346). It seems that such a message exists in the literature for young people, because it is also used by other authors, including Eva Ibbotson (2014) or Katherine Rundell (2017). Ibbotson's book presents events from the beginning of the 20th century – an orphan girl is sent from England to distant relatives in Brazil, and there she has the opportunity to meet not only the Indigenous inhabitants of the Amazon but also the son of a local herb seeker, who resembles people like E. Schultes. In the novel, the protagonist – similar to the protagonist described by Hussey – also reads Bates and Wallace's reports and meets locals: along with three companions, she goes to the village of the fictional Xanti group, whose members are presented as "the kindest people [they] have ever met . . . and full of knowledge about healing" (Ibbotson 2014: 103, 198). During the protagonists' time spent in the village, the reader learns more about Xanti's customs: everyone lives peacefully working on their tasks, doing everyday work, such as hunting, preparing food, music, singing, taking care of children, collecting fruit and seeds, or arranging joyful celebrations . . . (Ibbotson 2014: 274–275). All these activities are presented as harmonious between people and the world and decorated with laughter. Moreover, the author emphasizes that Xanti are not warriors – they do not fight other groups or outsiders, and in the event of danger, they hide deeper in the forest. Therefore, the image is closely related to the concepts of balance, harmony, and peaceful attitude – an idyllic image is created of people living in harmony with each other and nature, for whom life is a river which one should follow along its current and not fighting it (Ibbotson 2014: 282). This imagery frequently appears in novels, and in addition to the ones previously mentioned, it's worth noting one by Jessica Khoury (2012), in which the Indigenous people are modeled on representatives of the Tupi Guarani linguistic group (the author mentions this in the afterword – Khoury 2012: 399), but apart from the single words used in the text, there are no major references to cultural issues. Initially, the novel's young protagonist considers the local residents to be indistinguishable, even in terms of gender – she finally notes that men and women differ in hair length (which women wear longer– Khoury 2012: 112). When the main character meets the leaders of a local group, they turn out to be three elderly people, richly decorated with animal feathers and teeth, and the woman between them has her face and forearms decorated with complex tattoos (Khoury 2012: 115). Researchers believe that the Amazonian tattooing is currently the oldest still practiced – the age of these practices is set at 7,000 years (Krutak 2013). In her novel, Khoury described tattoos covering the entire face and forearms of women, which is fictional, because the facial patterns in Tupi Guarani usually take the form of thin lines from the mouth to the ears and from the eyes to the temples, and name signs are tattooed on the forearms – creating complicated patterns would probably be impossible, even due to climatic conditions in which bacteria could quickly develop in damaged skin. However, introducing this element (to which there are no references later in the novel) is an interesting description of practices that not everyone expects in the Amazon. The Kaiabi group, which continues to practice this form of body decoration, inhabits the Brazilian region of Mato Grosso, and in particular Xingu Indigenous Park. Various groups from the surrounding areas were moved to the Park – for Kaiabi it was a new place and for a long time they did not want to abandon the lands traditionally belonging to them. The Villas Boas brothers, who were nominated for the Nobel Peace Prize in 1971 for their work (their approach to Indigenous people differed significantly from previous practices – they wanted to save the cultural diversity of the Amazon, and possible assimilation with the Brazilian nation was to take place under the conditions and at a pace set by the Indigenous people themselves) believed that the resettlement of Indigenous people to the Park was the only way to save them (at that time a Brazilian trans-Amazon route was created, which crossed the Indigenous lands). The history of these events is presented in the movie "Xingu" (Hamburger 2014), which focuses on describing the actions of the Villas Boas brothers, but also shows Indigenous peoples (including Kaiabi, Kalapalo, and Panará) from the Mato Grosso area. Like only few other analyzed texts, the movie "Xingu" presents local inhabitants as ordinary people who care about their families and want to live in peace – even though the events take place in the first half of the 20th century, when the Indigenous inhabitants of Mato Grosso lived the same as their ancestors for centuries (the Villas Boas brothers made contact with groups that were isolated up to that point), they are not shown as "strange" or "exotic". According to the photos taken during the brothers' journey, the people wear their ornaments, live in traditional houses, etc. (cf. Hemming 2003: 94–95); however, the visitors' reactions and their concern for the fate of the Indigenous people do not portray these peoples and their practices as alien, but rather as simply different. Since the initial meeting with Indigenous groups, the Villas

Boas brothers made peaceful contact with them (Hemming 2019: 11), learned local languages, and cared about maintaining traditions. A movie about their actions is certainly needed, because it shows such diverse relations between local residents and visitors from the dominant national culture.

There is also another movie taking place in the Xingu Reserve, this time showing the modernity, in which a young documentary filmmaker goes to a Toa Toari village to film traditional rituals (Dutilleux 2004). Over time, the filmmaker learns the language of his hosts and succumbs to certain customs. He also falls in love with the chief's daughter (probably to make this possibility plausible, the chief's daughter looks almost like a European, which definitely distinguishes her from the other characters of the film). The film begins with a remark that all the presented customs are real, and the entire story is based on facts. And indeed, many cultural elements have been faithfully reproduced, although they leave a great deal of dissatisfaction, because despite the fact that the inhabitants of the village are played by the real Toa Toari, their practices are shown fairly uniformly and without going deeper into their meaning. This is not the group's story, but the story of a European who came to the Amazon. Indigenous people – probably Kamaiurá judging from their characteristic appearance – are shown as ordinary people, but in their homes there is unusual sterility, women cover the intimate parts of the body, and all elements of everyday life are fully traditional. In one of the most interesting scenes, the chief enters the village on a bicycle (and later the main character delivers another bike for the shaman), but apart from that, there are no other influences of the present day in the settlement, which seems to be fictitious. Kamaiurá had their first contact in 1884 (Instituto Socioambiental n.d.1), so it does not seem likely that in the 20th century these people did not adapt any "western" items except for a bicycle and boat motors. On the other hand, it is interesting to see the social life taking place mainly in a large square surrounded by houses – this space, classified mainly as "masculine" (as opposed to the space in the house, which carries the characteristics of "feminine" – Instituto Socioambiental n.d.1), is used as a place for meetings, dancing, *Huka-Huka* wrestling, and visits of people from outside the village. In the film, basically all these events take place. People speak their language from the Tupi Guarani group, and in addition, the film uses French, Portuguese, and English. Despite the lack of depth, this film shows Kamaiurá in a positive way, only to a small extent romanticizing or idealizing them.

An interesting proposition of Ciro Guerra, the director of the previously described film "El Abrazo de la Serpiente" (2015), is his eight-part series "Frontera Verde" (Guerra 2019) made for the Netflix streaming platform. One might think that this production shows – as for example "Xingu" – customs and practices of the Indigenous inhabitants of the Brazilian-Colombian borderland; however, local groups were almost completely omitted in the series. Instead, the fictional communities were created, which entails some risk in terms of cultural cohesion. In the show, the main character is a detective from

Bogota, whose investigation leads her to a remote place where she comes from. Her story intertwines with the story of two local Indigenous persons from many years ago and fictional groups: Arupani, Ya'ikawa, or Yurumi. The motive of the story is to unravel the mystery of murders committed on four women, but the true mystery turns out to be the so-called Wanderers who – according to the legend presented in the series – were the first to leave the head of the anaconda, when in prehistoric times it descended from the Milky Way and moved through the tropical forest and populated it with individual groups (Guerra 2019, ep. 2, 00:12:08). The Wanderer's task is to protect the forest, and when their time is over, to train a successor and to turn into a tree (Guerra 2019, ep. 2, 00:4:40). The mythology created in the series is somewhat artificial, because it is not supported by actual traditions. Therefore, it reproduces the stereotypical, magical image of Indigenous – and yet, if the creators would have used the rich oral tradition of Witoto groups that actually live on the border between Brazil and Colombia, many elements of this series could gain coherence.

The stereotypical image of Indigenous is built in parallel to other stereotypes present in this production – for example, a Nazi soldier who is hungry for knowledge that gives power over the world and therefore wants to possess the heart of a Wanderer at all costs (which he literally does, by cutting out the heart of one of the main female characters). Such techniques mean that despite the fascinating subject matter and an interesting approach to it, the series loses its credibility. The producers of the series emphasize that they wanted to tell a story about the Amazonian understanding of spiritual eternity (Guerra 2019, 00:1:36). They also wanted to be realistic and therefore hired people living in the areas where the events take place – including local Indigenous persons (one of the important roles is played by Simon Bolívar, known from playing Karamakate in Guerra's "El Abrazo de la Serpiente" – 2015). In the series, it is also possible to hear the Indigenous languages of the Amazon. However, this is probably not enough, because if these elements would have been expanded to include local cultural issues, perhaps the Western recipient learned more about the mythology and customs of groups living in this area. Instead, the viewer got a confirmation of the stereotypical, magical, incomprehensible image of the Amazonian peoples.

In the series, attention is also drawn to the music created in the rhythm of the heartbeat, which reflects the main idea of the series: Amazon, as a network connecting everything that is alive, is the heart of the world and its destruction is associated with the destruction of all of us. Guerra emphasizes that

> being in the Amazon, working and creating there, is an experience that alters your whole way if seeing and understanding the world. It changes all of your deeply rooted ideas – you learn to see life in different way. It's really a life learning experience.
>
> (Guerra 2019, 00:5:57)

The Indigenous inhabitants of the Amazon are also sometimes used only as a background for events: in order to authenticate the presented events, some cultural texts about the region mention the real places or names of Indigenous groups, even if the rest does not refer to it at all – an example may be a book from the Harlequin series (Wicks 2018), in which the events concern romance, but before leaving for the Amazon, the characters talk about the location of planned activities on the border between Brazil, Venezuela, and Guyana, and about a group that lives there: Ingariko. This is the real name of people living in the vicinity of Mount Roraima – Ingarikó, of which there are currently just over a thousand people, together with Patamona and Akawaio belonging to a larger group called Kapon (Instituto Socioambiental n.d.2). The doctor from the novel flies to this group to help in treatment, but then the native theme becomes completely blurred in the narrative, because it is not in the center of the author's interest (and probably readers who expect something completely different from this type of literature).

Notes

1 In Huaorani group, grandchildren are often named by their grandparents by their own name, so it could theoretically be assumed that Moipa shown in the film is a descendant of Moipa from the 1930s, but it seems unlikely.
2 Awards at Crystal Heart Heartland Festival and Palm Beach International Film Festival for "Beyond the Gates of Splendor".
3 Casement's report was published in a blue cover – hence its colloquial name "Blue Book".
4 Many species of fish in the Amazon reproduce at the beginning of the rainy season, and therefore there are definitely fewer of them just before this period and they should not be caught (Ruffino and Isaac 1995: 41–45).
5 Antonio Bolívar passed away in May 2020 due to a SARS-CoV-2 infection during the global pandemic, becoming a symbol of the particular vulnerability of Indigenous inhabitants to complications from this disease and the lack of adequate medical assistance (Ovalle 2020).

References

Alès, C. (2013). System of Naming and Crealization: Authentic Acculturation and/or Authentic Tradition? The Yanomami Case. Tipití. *Journal of the Society for the Anthropology of Lowland South America*, 11(1), 35–50.
Allende, I. (2002). *La ciudad de las bestias*. Debolsillo.
Andujar, C. (2020). *The Yanomami Struggle*. The Fondation Cartier pour l'art contemporain.
Basso, E. (2002). https://pib.socioambiental.org/en/Povo:Kalapalo (accessed 5.01.2024).
BBC. (2020). https://www.bbc.com/news/av/stories-51021984 (accessed 22.02.2024).

Besette, C. (2008). *Yai Wanonabälewä: The Enemy God* [film]. USA. Gospel Communications International. Length: 93 minutes.
Bogumilski, K. (2017, April 9). The Lost City of Z – Review. *Kinofilia*. https://www.kinofilia.pl/2017/04/the-lost-city-of-z-recenzja.html (accessed 4.01.2024).
Borofsky, R. (2005). *Yanomami: The Fierce Controversy and What We Can Learn from It*. University of California Press.
Brown, P. (1995). *Beyond a Mountain Valley: The Simbu of Papua New Guinea*. University of Hawai'i Press.
Campbell, A.T. (1995). *Getting to Know Wai Wai: An Amazonian Ethnography*. Routledge.
Casement, R. (1912). *Correspondence on the Treatment of British Colonial Subjects and Native Indians Employed in the Collection of Rubber in the Putumayo District*. His Majesty Stationery Office.
Chagnon, N. (1968). *Yanomamö: The Fierce People*. Holt, Rinehart and Winston.
Chagnon, N. (1988). Life Histories, Blood Revenge and Warfare in a Tribal Population. *Science*, 239(4843), 985–992.
Chagnon, N. (2013). *Noble Savages: My Life Among Two Dangerous Tribes – the Yanomamo and the Anthropologists*. Simon & Schuster.
Chagnon, N., & Irons, W. (1979). *Evolutionary Biology and Human Social Behavior: An Anthropological Perspective*. Duxbury Press.
Collin, R. (2017, March 23). Transporting and Profound, The Lost City of Z is an Instant Classic. *The Telegraph*. https://www.telegraph.co.uk/films/0/lost-city-z-review-transporting-profound-piece-cinema/ (accessed 23.03.2024).
Creepy Jar. (2019). *Green Hell* [video game]. Poland.
Crystal Dynamics. (2018). *Shadow of the Tomb Raider*. Peruvian Jungle. Eidos Montreal.
Dargis, M. (2017, April 13). Review: Hearts of Darkness and Light in "Lost City of Z". *The New York Times*. https://www.nytimes.com/2017/04/13/movies/the-lost-city-of-z-review-charlie-hunnam.html (accessed 4.01.2024).
Dutilleux, J.P. (2004). *Amazon Forever* [film]. France. N/A. Length: N/A.
Echeverri, J.A. (2010). To Heal or to Remember: Indian Memory of the Rubber Boom and Roger Casement's "Basket of Life". *ABEI Journal*, 12, 49–64.
Elliot, E. (1957). *Through Gates of Splendor*. Harper & Brothers.
Flores, F.A. (1984). Notes on Some Medicinal and Poisonous Plants of Amazonian Peru. *Advances in Economic Botany*, 1, 1–8.
Foundation Cartier. (2020). https://www.fondationcartier.com/en/exhibitions/claudia-andujar-lalutteyanomami (accessed 14.02.2020).
Gaiman, N., & McKean, D. (1989). *Black Orchid* [DC comics]. New York. N/A.
Goffin, A.M. (1994). *The Rise of Protestant Evangelism in Ecuador, 1895–1990*. University of Florida Press.
Grann, D. (2009). *The Lost City of Z: A Tale of Deadly Obsession in the Amazon*. Random House.
Gray, J. (2016). *The Lost City of Z* [film]. USA. Amazon Studios. Length: 141 minutes.

Greenberg, M. (2018). In Politics if Not Art., Realism Trumps Magic for Mario Vargas Llosa. *The Times*, 13 March. https://www.nytimes.com/2018/03/13/books/review/mario-vargas-llosa-sabers-utopias-neighborhood.html (accessed 24.03.2020).

The Guardian. (2020). https://www.theguardian.com/artanddesign/2020/jan/29/claudia-andujar-photography-yanomami-brazil-jair-bolsonaro (accessed 11.01.2024).

Guerra, C. (2015). *El Abrazo de la Serpiente (Embrace of the Serpent)* [Film]. Colombia. Ciudad Lunar Producciones. Length: 125 minutes.

Guerra, C. (2019). *Frontera verde* [Netflix series]. Colombia. Dynamo. Length: N/A.

Hamburger, C. (2014). *Xingu* [film]. Brazil. Globo Films. Length: 102 minutes.

Hanbury-Tenison, R. (1982). *Aborigines of the Amazon Rainforest: The Yanomami*. Time Life Books.

Hanon, J. (2004). *Through the Gates of Splendor* [film]. USA. Every Tribe Entertainment. Length: 111 minutes.

Hanon, J. (2005). *End of the Spear* [film]. USA. Every Tribe Entertainment. Length: 108 minutes.

Hanon, J. (2007). *The Grandfathers* [film]. USA. Every Tribe Entertainment. Length: 122 minutes.

Hemming, J. (2003). *Die If You Must: Brazilian Indians in the Twentieth Century*. Macmillan.

Hemming, J. (2017, April 1). *The Lost City of Z is a Very Long Way from a True Story – and I Should Know*. The Spectator.

Hemming, J. (2019). *People of the Rainforest. The Villas Boas Brothers, Explorers and Humanitarians of the Amazon*. Hurst & Company.

Hergé. (1937). *Le aventures de Tintin*. Casterman Edition, pp. 6–8.

Hussey, C. (2005). *The Valley of Secrets*. Hodder Children's Books.

Ibbotson, E. (2014). *Journey to the River Sea*. MacMillan Children's Books.

Instituto Sociambiental. (n.d.1). *Povos Indígenas no Brasil*. https://pib.socioambiental.org/en/Povo:Kamaiur%C3%A1 (accessed 20.02.2024).

Instituto Sociambiental. (n.d.2). *Povos Indígenas no Brasil*. https://pib.socioambiental.org/en/Povo:Ingarik%C3%B3 (accessed 30.08.2019).

Kakutani, M. (2009, March 16). *An Explorer Drawn to and Eventually Swallowed by, the Amazon*. New York Times.

Kermode, M. (2016). Embrace of the Serpent Review – you will be Transported. *The Guardian*, 12 June 2016. https://www.theguardian.com/film/2016/jun/12/embrace-of-the-serpent-observer-review (accessed 20.02.2024).

Khoury, J. (2012). *Origin*. Penguin Group.

Kopenawa, D. (2010). https://www.youtube.com/watch?v=zoXd279JzRE (accessed 29.03.2020).

Kopenawa, D., & Albert, B. (2013). *The Falling Sky: Words of a Yanomami Shaman* (N. Elliot, trans.). Harvard University Press.

Krutak, L. (2013). *The Kayabi: Tattooers of the Brazilian Amazon*. https://www.larskrutak.com/the-kayabi-tattooers-of-the-brazilian-amazon (accessed 20.11.2023).

Llosa, M.V. (1989). *The Storyteller*. Farrar, Straus and Giroux, Helen Lane (1987. El Hablador. Seix Barral Biblioteca Breve).
Llosa, M.V. (2012). *The Dream of the Celt*. Faber and Faber (2010. El sueño del Celta. Alfaguara).
Lóránt, A. (2006). *Indiánok*. National Geographic.
Lóránt, A. (2007). *Wapponi*. Kossuth Kiadó.
The Lost City of Z. (2016). J. Gray (dir.) [film]. USA. Amazon Studios. Length: 141 minutes.
Louis, W.R. (1964). Roger Casement and the Congo. *Journal of African History*, 5(3), 99–120.
Manara, M. (2008). *HP et Giuseppe Bergman*. Les Humanoïdes Associés, SAS.
McCullough, S.B. (n/a). *An Interview with Cirro Gerra*. http://screenprism.com/insights/article/ask-the-director-how-does-embrace-of-the-serpent-pay-tribute-to-native-amaz (accessed 12.09.2019).
Ministerio de Cultura. (2019). Ocaina. Hijos de moo finora buinaima. [in:] *Caracterizaciones de los pueblos indígenas de Colombia*. Ministry of Culture of Colombia. http://www.mincultura.gov.co/prensa/noticias/Documents/Poblaciones/PUEBLO%20OCAINA.pdf (accessed 12.09.2019).
Navarro, B. (2014a). *Amazon Rainforest Magic: The adventures of Namowë, a Yanomami Boy*. Baham Books.
Navarro, B. (2014b). *Yanomami Children and their community in the Amazon* [short film]. https://www.youtube.com/watch?v=wpUyIVA_lew&t=491s&ab_channel=BarbaraCraneNavarro (accessed 02.02.2024).
Navarro, B. (2015). *Amazon Rainforest Magic: The adventures of Meromi, a Yanomami Girl*. Bham Books.
Navarro, B. (2018). *Yanomami Photo Album* [Online]. http://xavier-reinoso.com/yanomami/yanomami.html (accessed 20.02.2024).
Nelson, J. (n.d.). *Before they Pass Away* [Online exhibition]. https://www.jimmynelson.com/people/huaorani (accessed 22.12.2023).
NewsWire. (2011). https://www.newswire.com/the-grandfathers-dvd-q-a-with-jim/100837 (accessed 12.01.2024).
Nobel Prize. (2010). *Nobel Prize Website*. https://www.nobelprize.org/prizes/literature/2010/summary/ (accessed 24.03.2020).
Ogden, L., Hall, B., & Tanita, K. (2013). Animals, Plants, People and Things: A Review of Multispecies Ethnography. *Environment and Society*, 4, 5–24.
Olivares, G. (2006). *La Gran Final* [Film]. Spain. N/A. Length: N/A.
Ovalle, J. (2020). *Murió el actor Antonio Bolívar, protagonista del Abrazo de la Serpiente*. https://www.lafm.com.co/colombia/murio-el-actor-antonio-bolivar-protagonista-del-abrazo-de-la-serpiente (accessed 20.01.2024).
Oxford, P. (n.d.). *Huaorani* [Online exhibition]. https://peteoxford.photoshelter.com/gallery/Huaorani/G0000RXA8HboeJYo/C00009Z2XshtGaJo (accessed 13.10.2023).
Oxford, P., & Bish, R. (2009). *The Spirit of the Huaorani*. Imagine Publishing.
Patchett, A. (2011). *State of Wonder*. Bloomsbury.
Peluso, D. (2004). "That Which I Dream Is True": Dream Narratives in an Amazonian Community. *Dreaming*, 14(2–3), 107–119.
PIB. (n.d.). https://pib.socioambiental.org.br/en/Povo:Xingu (accessed 02.02.2024).

PluggedIn. (n.d.). https://www.pluggedin.com/movie-reviews/yaiwanonablew theenemygod (accessed 24.02.2024).
Pollak, S. (2016). Why Roger Casement is still Remembered by the People of the Amazon. *The Irish Times*.
Raleigh, W. (1595). *The Discovery of Guiana*. https://www.gutenberg.org/files/2272/2272-h/2272-h.htm#link2H_4_0004 (accessed 11.01.2024).
Rollins, J. (2002). *Amazonia*. William Morrow.
Rose, P., & Conlon, A. (1983). *Yanomamo* [musical]. Prod. Weinberger. London.
Ruffino, M.L., & Isaac V.J. (1995). Life Cycle and Biological Parameters of Several Brazilian Amazon Fish Species. *Naga, the ICLARM Quarterly*, 18(4), 41–45.
Rundell, K. (2017). *The Explorer*. Bloomsbury.
ScreenPrism. (n.d.). *Interview with Cirro Gerra*. http://screenprism.com/insights/article/ask-the-director-how-does-embrace-of-the-serpent-pay-tribute-to-native-amaz (accessed 12.09.2019).
Slovenski Etnografski Muzej. (2011a). *The Cosmic Anaconda* [exhibition]. Arte Amazonia, part of the Orinoco: Indians of the Amazon Rainforest Exhibition by the Cisneros.
Slovenski Etnografski Muzej. (2011b). https://www.youtube.com/watch?v=1WGJfnsDWmE 0:56 (accessed 04.03.2020).
Steam. (2018). https://steamcommunity.com/app/815370/discussions/0/1739964947811903433/ (accessed 05.01.2024).
Stein, S. (2016). Embrace of the Serpent – a Tale of Metamorphosis. *Cultural Daily*, 26 February. https://culturaldaily.com/embrace-serpent-tale-metamorphosis/ (accessed 20.02.2024).
Super Express. (2018). https://www.se.pl/wiadomosci/gwiazdy/obrzydliwe-zadanie-w-ameryka-express-chicha-przyprawila-gwiazdy-o-mdlosci-aa-YV5C-VmU8-5WzR.html (accessed 04.01.2024).
Survival International. (2013). https://assets.survivalinternational.org/documents/891/2-2013-anthropologists-letter.pdf (accessed 29.08.2019).
Survival International. (n.d.1). https://www.survivalinternational.org/articles/3130-sydney-possuelo-experiences-of-contact (accessed 5.01.2024).
Survival International (n.d.2). https://www.survivalinternational.org/material/28 (accessed 29.08.2019).
Thacker, N. (2016). *The Amazon Code* (Kindle edition). Turtleshell Press.
TVN. (2018). *America Express* [Television program]. Poland.
Weibel, P. (2010). *Amazonas. Music Theater in Three Parts* [Theatrical performance]. Zentrum für Kunst und Medientechnologie Karlsruhe, Goethe-Institut, Teatro Nacional de São Carlos, Yanomami-Organisation Hutukara.
Whitten, N.E. (1976). *Sacha Runa: Ethnicity and Adaptation of Ecuadorian Jungle Quichua*. University of Illinois Press.
Wicks, B. (2018). *Tempted by Her Hot-Shot Doc*. Harlequin Mills & Boon Limited.
Wierucka, A. (2015). *Huaorani of the Western Snippet*. Palgrave.
Wilbert, J. (ed.). (1994). *Encyclopedia of World Cultures*. G.K. Hall & Company.

Yost, J. (1981). People of the Forest [in:] *Ecuador in the Shadow of the Volcanoes*, ed. P. Gordon-Warren, & S. Curl. Libri Mundi.

Zentrum für Kunst und Medientechnologie. (2010). *Karlsruhe*. https://zkm.de/en/project/amazonas (accessed 11.01.2023).

Ziegler-Otero, L. (2007). *Resistance in an Amazonian Community: Huaorani Organizing against the Global Economy*. Berghain Books.

Shamanism

Shamanism continues to evoke profound fascination and strong emotional responses in the Western world when exploring non-European cultural practices. It is still mysterious, not fully explained and disputable, and yet it was practiced (and partly still is) on almost all continents. Today, the term "shamanism" covers many different activities, although the word itself comes from Siberia and should define only what it means in the culture of Evenks, that is, "a man of power" (Vitebsky 1996: 10) in their own community. However, it is worth noting that the term "shamanism" has been adapted and utilized with various meanings in contemporary discourse, becoming a common and widely used term in many contexts today. Shamans hold the belief that alongside our physical world, there exists a parallel supernatural realm inhabited by spiritual beings. According to their beliefs, these supernatural beings possess the ability to interact with and potentially cause harm to human souls. In each community, it is typically the shaman who is able to access the supernatural realm and establish communication with or confront spiritual beings. The shaman achieves this by entering a different state of consciousness, often referred to as a trance state. Through this altered state of consciousness, the shaman can provide assistance to their community by interacting with and addressing spiritual entities. Depending on the culture, shamans achieve a trance state in different ways. Some use hallucinogens (e.g., Sacha Runa from South America – Whitten 1976: 40), drum sounds (e.g., Siberian shamans from Tuva, Asia – Kenin-Lopsan 1997: 111), a combination of these methods (e.g., Buryats from Asia – Neumann Fridman 2004: 94), and there are also communities in which a shaman uses only his own song to enter into a trance (e.g., Huaorani people from South America – Wierucka 2015: 163). Nowadays, there are problems with the definition of the word "shaman" due to the variety of practices and meanings, but it can probably be agreed that

> a shaman knows the spirit world and human soul through "ecstasy", the power of an altered state of consciousness, or trance, which is used to

make a connection to the world of the spirits in order to bring about benefits to the community.

(Walter and Neumann Fridman 1994: xi)

This definition therefore excludes both the so-called neo-shamanists who use native shamanic techniques for personal purposes (such as "discovering their own subconscious"), as well as artists who believe that during the creative process their mind functions in a different state of consciousness. However, as practice has shown, the word "shaman" is misunderstood and abused (e.g., Tantra n.d.).

Individuals who become shamans often undergo similar experiences during their journey. One such characteristic occurrence is known as the "shaman's disease". This condition is marked by a profound illness that brings the individual to the brink of death, ultimately enabling them to access and harness special powers. Accounts of the "shaman's disease" have been documented in various parts of the world, and it typically serves as the defining element through which a community identifies a future shaman (Vitebsky 1996: 58–59).

Shamanism is very diverse in the Amazon – it would seem that groups living in a similar environment and neighboring ones will also have similar shamanistic practices, but of course this is not the case. It is enough to compare, for instance Huaorani, Yanomami, Runa, or Shuar people, to note that contact with the supernatural world is completely different for them: some shamans from these groups use hallucinogens, others do not, hallucinogens are taken in various forms, some use special attributes in their work, etc. In this situation, it is difficult to talk about "Amazonian shamanism" – rather, as in the case of other regions, one should talk about "shamanisms" or call these practices and people representing them with appropriate terms from the language used by the group (in this case, e.g., in Huaorani, it will be *miñe* or *ydo* – Wierucka 2015: 96, in Shuar *iwishin* – Centro Yachak 2012, and in Runa *yachay* – Whitten 1976: 142). Nevertheless, there are some common elements that are characteristic for the region's practices. One of them is the use of hallucinogenic drugs to enter into a trance (there are exceptions to this practice, but if one considers Amazonian shamanism in general, the use of these drugs is very common). Many plants containing various hallucinogenic compounds grow in the tropical forest – the most commonly used is *ayahuasca* (*Banipteriopsis caapi*), which is used to make an infusion. Usually, the shaman and his patient reach a state of trance after ingestion of *ayahuasca*, and then the treating person is able to see the disease in the patient's body and remove it. He is then also able to negotiate with or fight the spiritual beings causing the disease. Often, however, other treatments are used first, such as "cleansing" by fumigating the patient with tobacco smoke and using a special "broom" made of leaves to chase away any possibly harmful spiritual beings. Shamans possess extensive knowledge of the forest and its medicinal plants, and they often incorporate herbal medicine into their practices. They utilize their understanding of the natural environment to identify and harness the healing properties of various plants. This allows them to utilize herbal remedies as a vital component of their healing and spiritual practices. When the above methods fail, the shaman uses *ayahuasca* and enters into a trance, looking for the cause of the disease.

In his theory of "*ayahuasca* shamanism", Peter Gow explores the potential existence of shamanistic practices that predate colonization, particularly prior to the arrival of missionaries. He delves into the notion that Indigenous cultures may have had their own distinct forms of shamanism that were practiced prior to external influences. According to him, shamanism using *ayahuasca* developed on the basis of previous practices only in the encounter of Indigenous people with the Christian ideology in the mission area (Gow 1996: 107). This may be evidenced by the similarity of the elements of the *ayahuasca* ritual to the elements of the mass in the Christian church and the lack of these practices in groups that experienced contact with the Western culture late). The widespread use of *ayahuasca* in the Amazon region can be attributed to the expansion of the rubber tree juice harvest, commonly referred to as the rubber boom, during the 19th century. This phenomenon led to the practice of *ayahuasca* spreading across a vast area of the Amazon basin. Furthermore, Gow suggests that *ayahuasca* shamanism in the past centuries might not have primarily revolved around disease treatment, contrary to its current emphasis. The author supports this argument by providing examples of Indigenous groups that had late contact with outside influences. In these cases, the role of the shaman encompassed activities such as locating wild animals for hunting, interpreting dreams, and gathering information about the present, past, or future during trance states. This implies that the functions and focus of *ayahuasca* shamanism may have evolved over time. However, his historical considerations do not change the fact that shamanism using the *ayahuasca* ritual has been very widespread in the Amazon basin for almost two centuries.

A distinctive characteristic of shamanistic practices in the Amazon region is the symbolic significance attributed to the jaguar. The jaguar holds a prominent place in the symbolism and mythology associated with shamanism in the Amazon. It is often regarded as a powerful and transformative animal spirit, embodying qualities such as strength, agility, and mystical prowess within the spiritual realm. The jaguar's symbolism plays a significant role in shaping the beliefs and practices of Amazonian shamanism – special powers are attributed to this animal and shamans often benefit from its help (e.g., in some groups, there is a belief that shamans transform into jaguars; in others, shamans wander with jaguar spirits during a trance, etc. – Walter and Neumann Fridman 1994: 257; Vitebsky 1996: 46; Fausto 2004: 158).

Amazonian shamans are most often described as "healers" (their positive social, therapeutic, and integrative roles are emphasized – Brown 1989: 8), and of course this is largely true, but another aspect of their activity should not be avoided. Many shamans are classified as *dark shamans*, using their powers to bring diseases or other misfortunes. The ability to heal and harm is also associated with ambiguous morality (Whitehead and Wright 2004: 10). Therefore, shamans are usually surrounded by respect, but also fear, although often dark shamans are not fully recognized (a given group does not always know who has such powers, although sometimes the same shaman may play both roles depending on the circumstances). Hence the division of diseases into those that are caused by the action of a shaman and others, one could say natural (although, for example, often a snake bite can be treated as a result of an activity of a shaman, so the division is often not fully clear). Shamanism is much more however: it involves knowledge, healing, and power, and it is ambiguous by nature (Narby and Huxley 2004: 7).

In Europe, from the beginning of geographic discoveries and later colonization, shamanism was seen as an activity of the devil – communicating with spiritual beings to heal or retrieve life teachings was not within the Christian framework of approaching life and religion. The initial accounts of the Indigenous inhabitants in the Amazon region often depicted them as devil worshippers engaged in practices that were astonishing to the newcomers. These early narratives described unfamiliar rituals and ceremonies that were viewed through the lens of the colonizers' cultural perspectives and interpretations. These depictions reflected the lack of understanding and misinterpretation of the Indigenous spiritual practices, leading to the characterization of them as devil worship. In 1535, Gonzalo Fernandez de Oviedo described shamans as people who did not know God, worshipping the Devil who spoke through them (Oviedo 2004: 12). Similar descriptions were provided by André Thévet, a French priest in 1557 (2004: 13), or Antoine Biet in 1664 (Biet 2004: 16); therefore in Europe, the image of shamanistic practices as related to Satan was systematically perpetuated. These descriptions related to South America, which is why I cited them here, but the idea of shamanism as contact with demons was found by explorers around the world. In the 17th century, the Russians came across the word *saman/shaman* in Siberia, describing people dealing with practices related to specific power and contact with the supernatural world, and shortly afterwards, the use of this word spread not only among travelers but also later in science. During the 18th century, a period marked by Enlightenment ideas and intellectual pursuits, shamanic practices did not receive significant attention or exploration. They were most often referred to as "tricks and performances" that did not have much to do with knowledge (Narby and Huxley 2004: 2), but at the turn of the 18th century, German researchers popularized the term "schamanism" among representatives of Western culture (Znamenski 2007: 6). Meanwhile, Richard Spruce, an English botanist (whom I mentioned in the chapter regarding the history of exploration of the Amazon region), described, among others, the *ayahuasca* vine and its use in shamanistic practices (Narby and Huxley 2004:

2). Wacław Sieroszewski, a writer and researcher of Siberia at the turn of the 19th century, described three types of shamans present there: "ordinary" (with little power), "great" (having great power) and "last" (referred to by the author as weirdos, half-crazed – Sieroszewski 1935: 358). The description of a shaman as "deranged person" was already popular at that time. Along with the development of various sciences, including psychology and psychoanalysis, in the 19th century shamans were considered to have mental problems. Shamanism was often analyzed from a psychological point of view and treated as "an unfortunate product of primitive minds – and that of disturbed minds" (Walsh 2010: 88). This was most likely due to the fact that both the trance and spiritual beings occurring in the shamanic reality were not acceptable to the Western culture. This could not be described in rational frameworks and was therefore perceived as a mental disorder of individual shamans. Such an opinion remained for quite a long time. In 1956, George Devereux, a psychoanalyst and anthropologist, wrote explicitly that "a shaman is mentally insane.... To say it briefly, there is no reason not to treat the shaman as a deeply neurotic and psychotic figure" (Devereux 2004: 120).

The negative opinion about shamans was a derivative of the Western rationalist-positivist ideology adopted as the norm by which other cultural practices were judged. In this context, everything that was non-European appeared to be an abnormal expression of a bad assessment of reality (Walsh 2010: 90).

Numerous field studies, scientific articles, and lectures in the 20th century began to present the diversity of shamanistic practices, as well as their importance. In 1951, Mircea Eliade's ground-breaking book was published, describing similarities in the behavior and symbolism of these practices around the world. According to Eliade, shamanism consists of magical, mystic, and religious practices (Eliade 1974: xxv). His work, which aimed to find a place for shamanism in the history of religion, has already been criticized many times (mainly due to the fact of collecting data, as the author did not work with shamans, did not attend rituals, and the data came from the accounts of others), but it is still an important element in the anthropological construction of understanding the phenomenon of shamanism (Wallis 2003: 35).

Scientific knowledge of shamanism began to appear in popular culture in the 1960s, mainly through the works of Carlos Castaneda, which became bestsellers (Castaneda 1968 and others). Castaneda described his experiences while studying with a shaman from the Yaqui tribe in Mexico. The author was an anthropologist and conducted his field research as part of his master's thesis. The result of this research was knowledge about shamanistic practices, but also about the way of perceiving the world, which in the 1960s and 1970s fell on very fertile ground. After all, this is the period of the hippie movement expressed through such things as rebellion against the unified experience of life or attempts of using various hallucinogens and drugs. In this context, the teachings of Don Juan, the shaman of Yaqui, became a justification for various actions, and the author of the books himself became a sort of a chosen one and a guru. The fact that Castaneda most likely wrote fiction instead of scientific work did not prevent thousands of his "followers" from learning from him (Znamenski 2007: 207). The world of science initially accepted Castaneda's work with confidence, but later its scientific side was undermined. It is also worth emphasizing that with his texts, Castaneda brought the ideas of shamanism closer to the average reader, mainly due to the accessible language devoid of scientific binding. All this has contributed to the emergence of the neo-shamanistic movement, which uses traditional practices in isolation from the cultural context, so that a given individual can reach their subconscious during a trance, get to know their "true self".

The next step to popularize shamanism was its idealization. It was believed (and in circles associated with neo-shamanism it is still believed to this day) that shamans know the "truth" about life, that they are guides to the real and supernatural world. This approach, however, does not take on the dark side of shamanism. Besides, neo-shamanism usually chooses only those elements that suit its practitioners in their own imagination.

Neo-shamanism and its various iterations are not the primary focus of my inquiry here. However, it is important to acknowledge that they have played a significant role in popularizing traditional shamanistic practices within the Western world. In today's society, much of the general knowledge about shamanism is derived from workshops, gatherings, or sessions that often diverge from the authentic practices and understanding of shamanism within Indigenous cultures.

Today, the situation of Amazonian shamans is complex. Many practices have been lost, some are still ongoing, although often in a revised or simplified version. The treatment provided by shamans continued to hold cultural significance, and one of the reasons for this was the limited accessibility to Western-style medical treatments over the years. The sense of inner local belonging of shamans has also changed. Today they are organized at provincial, regional, and national levels. For example, the first national shaman convention in Ecuador was held in Ambato in November 2001, and the first international one – in Santo Domingo de los Colorados in July 2002 (Whitten 2003: 253).

With the change of laws (previously prohibiting shamanistic practices) and the possibility of celebrating rituals, new opportunities have opened up for other activities that were not previously foreseen: for example, the so-called *ayahuasca* tourism or stands for shamans on ethnic marketplaces. When visiting one of such stands, you can buy tropical seed jewelry, while another offers traditional meal made of *mayun* (beetle larvae), or you can undergo the ritual of purification carried out by *yachay*. Shallowing the meaning of shamans for the local community by organizing trips to perform the *ayahuasca* ritual for tourists, for instance, is the result of rapid growth of tourism. This topic is not a part of the subject of this book, but it should be mentioned that today's tourism has a very significant impact on all cultural practices (including shamanism). People visiting the Amazon region, coming from different parts of the world want to experience what they have read or watched, and – quite paradoxically – the locals provide it because they know the expectations of the visitors. Thus, a vicious circle of demand and supply arises, in which both sides are deluded that what they watch or present is "authentic" (Wierucka 2018: 98). This is particularly important in the case of shamanism, since the above-mentioned "*ayahuasca* tourism" also affects the local perception of these practices.

*

In widely available cultural texts, shamanism is often portrayed in two main ways. First, it is depicted as an enigmatic practice, characterized by its status as "secret knowledge" that is difficult to comprehend fully. Second, it is often associated with healing, particularly in the context of herbal medicine and natural remedies. This portrayal tends to focus on the practical aspects of shamanism, emphasizing its therapeutic and medicinal aspects rather than its spiritual or metaphysical dimensions. For example, in the children's book "The Vanishing Rainforest" (Platt and van Wyk 2004), the shaman is portrayed as a healer who recognizes malaria and sends the main character on a quest to find the "bitter vine bark". Interestingly, malaria comes from Africa and was brought to the Amazon region by the colonists, and the shamans did not know how to deal with it because it was not known to them before. The fact that the shaman knows which plant (containing alkaloids, including probably quinine – Countinho 2013) should be used to treat malaria may indicate his contacts with representatives of Western culture – probably missionaries. In this book, the shaman also consults spiritual beings, but he himself states that no one was ill with malaria before the *nabë* ("strangers") came, so spiritual beings will not help here. The shaman in this story about the village of Yanomami appears only for the moment of a child's illness. He has no other role to fulfill, he is not shown as an important member of the group, and his practices are described marginally.

The authors of "The Shaman's Apprentice" (Cherry and Plotkin 2001) children's book approach the issue of shamanism in a different way, which probably results primarily from their background – Mark Plotkin is an ethnobotanist who worked in the Amazon rainforest for many years and to some extent was a student of the shaman himself (Plotkin 1993). The story is about the value of traditional medicine and the role of the shaman in the society. The main character is a boy admiring a shaman, even though he has lost his place in the community, because the missionaries proclaimed that his knowledge is no longer needed due to medicines imported from outside. As proof of this, the missionaries provided the people with a cure for malaria, which the shamans were unable to provide. In the rest of the story, community learns that the drug comes from a tropical forest and was discovered by Indigenous people who know the forest and its resources very well. Over time, knowledge and respect for the shaman are restored, and the main character becomes his apprentice, so traditional healing practices will be passed on to subsequent generations. The book, which is the author's own reflection on his own experiences among the Tirió, limits the role of the shaman only to herbal medicine. His expeditions to find leaves, roots, or bark are emphasized, from which he then prepares medicinal infusions. However, the actions of the shaman in this group are in fact more serious: he is also the intermediary between the world of reality perceived by the senses and the supernatural world inhabited by spiritual beings. At the same time, he is a doctor, clergyman, pharmacist, psychiatrist, as well as a priest dealing with leading souls into the afterlife, and other things (Plotkin 1993: 96). Perhaps the authors jointly decided that the subject wider than herbal medicine would not be suitable for children. It is a pity, because since the expert dealt with shamanism, he could show how complex and ambiguous it is.

An interesting picture of shamanistic practices and the process of moving away from them are also presented in the film titled "Yai Wanonabälewä: The Enemy God" (Besette 2008), described in the previous chapter. At this point, I would like to analyze the unusual representation of shamanism, which appears as an immanent part of culture. The main character of the film, called Shake, is a shaman who is still in the process of learning. His slightly older brother-in-law is already a recognized shaman with great powers, and he provides teachings to Shake. During the film, a family of missionaries comes to the village to talk about Great Spirit, a Christian god, and the first problems appear in this context. Shamans talk to each other about Yai Wanonabälewä, the great evil spirit to be avoided. Each shaman has his own spiritual beings with whom he works, but this one is described as extremely strong and encouraging evil actions. In the course of the film, Yai Wanonabälewä turns out to be a Christian god "good and full of love", who, however, recommends abandoning polygamy and other cultural practices, as well as abandoning the pursuit of bloody revenge.

The Yanomami shamanism, as in other groups of the region, is based on belief in spiritual beings, spirits – they can serve the shaman (then they are called *hekula dibi*), but they can also be hostile (*sai dibi*), which can be sent by other shamans and cause illness (Ramos 1995: 161) or death. Yanomami believed that death is most often the result of the action of a person (it was possible to kill, e.g., by using "magic plants", killing the animal spirit of the victim or using soil from the footsteps of the victim – Ramos 1995: 161). In Yanomami's life, spiritual beings determined the fate of man and his actions (e.g., the above-mentioned animal spirit, *nonoshi*, was an *alter ego* of a person (Ramos 1995: 164), and its killing caused immediate death of a human being). Shamans were able to see spiritual beings in a trance and remedy their actions with the help of their *hekula dibi*, which they hold in their chests. *Hekula dibi* are recruited from the spirits of the dead, who have been possessed by a shaman (Ramos 1995: 171). In order to enter the supernatural world, the shaman takes hallucinogenic agents, in the case of Yanomami *yãkoana* (Kopenawa 2013: 78) – powder (its power depends on what it was prepared out of), which is blown in through a nasal tube and quickly absorbed through the mucosa. A hallucinogenic agent induces visual experiences and altered states of consciousness, during which shamans engage in battles or seek guidance from spiritual entities.

Shamanism in Besset's film is shown not only faithfully but is also visualized. Spiritual beings appear in the visions of the main character in human form; they materialize in the village or in the forest; and they make voices heard by the shaman. Practices such as holding spirits in the chest, taking *yãkoana* or healing are presented reliably and with the traditional elements for Yanomami. In this context, the shaman's black hip band appears somewhat comical, setting him apart from the other settlement inhabitants who are dressed in red. However, this minor detail pales in comparison to the overall portrayal of shamanism in the film. When the family of missionaries introduces the idea of a Christian god, the main character refuses to accept the Great Spirit, arguing that there is no place in his heart for more spiritual beings, but he is convinced that the new spirit is better than all the others (Besette 2008, 01:12:26). For this reason, he gets rid of all his spiritual beings and accepts a Christian god. This leads to a fierce discussion between him and his teacher, who has passed on all his knowledge. The missionaries in the film are shown casually, almost as if they did not have any impact on the changes taking place in the village, and yet they used the traditional belief in spiritual beings to convince the shaman and other inhabitants to accept a god, whom they called *great spirit* and presented as having greater power than all spiritual beings that have helped communities so far. In a scene from the 1990s, Shake says to his family that "the supernatural beings we called friends deceived us". In his understanding, the tradition of seeking bloody revenge is believed to stem from the influence of vengeful spirits, whereas the teachings of the Christian God promote peaceful life and suggest that it is superior (Besette 2008, 01:15:10). At the end of the film, the main character asks God for help in preventing another bloodshed and states that even if it does not work, he will not bring back his spiritual beings. As a result, there is an image of a shaman who believes in a Christian god and at the same time does not deny the existence of other supernatural beings. This can be clearly seen in the last scene of the film, when the inhabitants of the settlement enter the church, and the shot moves to the forest, where spirits can be heard. It should be kept in mind that it is the shaman's story, his vision of history, so this ending is not irrelevant. The film is credible with the presentation of the real hero of the story at the beginning of the film and the commentary about him at the end. Today, Shake "still tells the story of his freedom" (Besette 2008, 01:39:20). While not questioning the authenticity of the shaman's personal account, one may ponder why he embraced the new faith and turned away from shamanism. From a young age, he was aware of his destined path to become a shaman, but he encountered difficulties and conflicts along the way. His teacher

Shaping the image of Amazonian Indigenous people   63

persuaded him several times that he would be able to control spiritual beings, assuring him that he would succeed. At the same time, Shake was tempted by Yai Wanonabälewä to become the greatest of all possible shamans, the one who takes souls. At this stage Shake believes that Yai Wanonabälewä is a demon, an evil spirit with great power and only later is the situation reversed and he becomes a Christian god. However, it is then that a kind of loop closes and Shake takes souls. He refuses to accept spiritual beings and work with them to benefit his group; he does not assimilate ancestral spirits, although apparently he still believes in their existence. They are in the forest, they are in the vicinity, and Shake resists their powers. He did not resist the Christian god – after all, he is a *great spirit*, so maybe he was too weak of a shaman. His brother-in-law defends his spiritual beings to the end and does not allow a great spirit to reach him. After all, he is a shaman of great power.

The review of the film, which appeared on one of the Christian blogs, speaks of showing "demonic ceremonies and healing, which consist of singing, dancing and hallucinogenic drugs" (PluggedIn n.d.), but such an opinion is not surprising due to the authors' view of the world. For them, the introduction of Christianity is probably the only possible way of "development" (they mention showing "negative elements revealing how much the Yanomami need the intervention of God" in the film). James Yost, a well-known anthropologist and researcher of Amazonian cultures, approaches the spiritual world differently: in his statement, he first emphasizes that the film "Yai Wanonabälewä" shows how real the world of spiritual beings is to the inhabitants of the Amazon region – it is not just an image, but a real part of their world (Yost 2010).

To some extent, this is shown by the action of Isabel Allende's novel "La Cuidad de las Bestias" (2002) – a shaman in the Yanomami group always appears accompanied by his spiritual partner, a girl who died half a century earlier, but due to the love for the shaman remained with him in the form of a spirit. The shaman himself is described as an old man wearing a short plant apron, necklaces made of shells, seeds, and animal teeth (so quite stereotypically) and having in-depth knowledge of both past and future events. During the protagonists' visit to the village of Yanomami, the Walimai shaman relieves the tension created by the death of the chief and prepares *ayahuasca* (also called "magic potion" in the novel), which all men in the settlement take, because they must "look into their hearts" to choose a new chief (Allende 2002: 89). The novel also features *yopo* ("magic ceremonial powder", or the above-mentioned *yãkoana*) blown into the nose to achieve the state of trance – and this is a hallucinogenic agent actually used by Yanomami, while *ayahuasca* was probably added here to make the story more attractive, because this ethnic group does not use it. Among the protagonists there is *a curandero*, that is, a person treating his fellow tribesmen, and although he is not called a shaman, the described actions indicate shamanistic practices, such as sucking out bad elements sent by spirits from the patient's body (Allende 2002: 89).

Therefore, some threads are mixed here, but this does not change the fact that Yanomami shamanism is shown without seeking sensation, as a cultural practice, which the characters (and the reader) do not understand, but accept as an important element of the culture of the group in which they found themselves.

Yanomami shamanism is also depicted (but very marginally) in James Rollins's novel "Amazonia" (2002) – one of the depicted Americans is initiated as a shaman, because the shaman of the local group predicts his own upcoming death. The ritual is presented according to the Yanomami tradition: after blowing a hallucinogenic agent into the nose of the future shaman and the current shaman, the latter leads the American through a shamanic journey full of visions of spiritual beings and explanations of the functioning of the local group (Rollins 2002: 420). Apart from this one scene in the novel, there is no more information about Yanomami's spiritual life, which probably results from the sensational character of the novel and the context of the presented events.

Shamanistic practices by Yanomami have also been introduced to art in the form of film, installation, and photography: French artist Barbara Navarro uses various artistic forms to express the complex process of trance and communication with spiritual beings. For example, in her installation titled "The Way of the Shaman" (Navarro 2012b) the artist presented the relations between heaven and earth and the exchange of energy between them by suspending long vertical bands symbolizing the vision of Yanomami cosmos. The installation is three-dimensional, so it allows the recipient to enter the center of the cosmic world and experience a different look at it. An interesting project is also a series of photographs under the joint title "Shamanic Trance" (Navarro 2012a), in which shamanic faces are processed with various artistic filters, giving them a supernatural character, thus expressing the encounters of shamans with spiritual beings, whose presence is shown by manipulations in portrait photographs. Navarro also uses the technique of overlapping shots, which allows her to achieve the effect of unusualness and, again, the presence of something impossible to see in other ways. Both works – the installation and the series of photographs – are combined in a short film showing the activities of the Yanomami shaman during trance and contact with the supernatural world, as well as filtered photos of the shamans' faces (Navarro 2014). The film brings the viewer's experience to the physiological level. The installation and photos are of a slightly different nature, but all three elements complement each other well, giving the viewer a multifaceted idea of this shamanistic practice.

The vision of two parallel worlds, of which the invisible one is more real for us, as in the "Yai Wanonabälewä" movie, is presented in the film titled "Embrace of the Serpent" (Guerra 2015). The main character in the film is the shaman Karamakate, whose encounters with European researchers occur with a time gap of half a century. A shaman passes on some of his knowledge on to the travelers and he emphasizes that "every plant, every tree, every flower is full of wisdom" (Guerra 2015, 01:02:08), and that this wisdom can be accessed through them. However, he notes that newcomers are unable to do so because they perceive the world differently. Karamakate is shown as a healer who knows old treatments and also uses *ayahuasca* known as *caapi*.

The titular snake is also associated with the practice of shamanism. Among the Amazon groups, there are various myths associated with it, and in particular this applies to boa (*Boa sp.*) and anaconda (*Eunectes sp.*). For example, in Barasano tales from Brazil and Colombia, the mythological anaconda ancestor swam down the river, placing his sons, human beings, on the ground (Overing Kaplan 1981: 157). In Ecuador, among Quichua, the anaconda is the embodiment of Sungui, the water spirit Master, and in the myth of Huaorani, the anaconda is one of the causes of existence of the *cohuori*, that is, aliens, people other than Huaorani (Wierucka 2015: 49). The myth of Manchineri from Brazil, in turn, tells the story of a boa, whose coexistence with a young woman led to a destructive flood. At the end of the myth, the woman gives birth to the first man, Tslatu (Virtanen 2015: 96). A boa along with the jaguar are the strongest non-human characters in the cosmology of the Amazon groups – boa is the "mother" of all aquatic beings (Roe 1982). During the trance, shamans can communicate with the spirit of a boa or anaconda, and the same happens in "Embrace of the Serpent". Karamakate, the shaman of the Cohiuano group presented in the film, takes the researcher on a spiritual journey. In the last scenes, he gives him the *medora caapi*, the variety of vine containing the strongest hallucinogenic compounds according to the protagonist, which existed "before the snake descended" (Guerra 2015, 01:53:37). The shaman warns the European that the anaconda he encounters will be fearsome, but he advises him not to be afraid. Instead, he instructs him to surrender himself to her embrace, as she will then lead him to ancient realms devoid of life (Guerra 2015, 01:54:12). Karamakate instructs the researcher to bring back the story of what he witnessed and experienced to his homeland. He urges him to share this story through a song, emphasizing that by doing so, the researcher will become fully human. This will only be possible if he shares what he has learnt with others. The protagonist (previously mentioned Richard Schultes, researcher of the hallucinogenic agents of the Amazon), accepts *caapi*. He has visions of "time before time" (this is the only colorful element of the film – visions are saturated with color and shown in slow motion), sees the forest, star clusters, galaxies, atoms, to finally wake up alone on a hill, with a dying fire, with Karamakate's necklace in his hand. The world to which the researcher went during the trance is a parallel world, which is perceived by shamans. Although we see the shaman all the time in the reality of researchers, he repeatedly emphasizes that this is only one of the possibilities and that the world perceived by the senses is not absolute and certain. The figure of Karamakate is very calm, closed, confident in its actions and knowledge of his ancestors – this is probably how we would like to imagine shamans not only of the Amazon region. The protagonist arouses respect of both strangers and local residents, and the actions he takes are crucial for the presented events. As I mentioned in the previous chapter, the film was produced on cooperation with the Indigenous people, and many of them are actors in it. Therefore, the shamanistic practices and other aspects of the depicted culture are portrayed with accuracy. Although the film is a work of fiction, it incorporates numerous authentic cultural elements from the region where the story is set.

The figure of a shaman similar to Karamakate appears in Charmian Hussey's novel (Hussey 2005). The main character possesses extraordinary abilities that enable them to establish communication with spiritual entities and also possesses extensive knowledge regarding the medicinal properties of plants (Hussey 2005: 275). The shaman is highly respected by the entire community and serves as a role model for the fellow residents. However, the novel does not delve into the shamanistic aspect in detail because most of the events happen in modern times, and the reader only learns about the Indigenous peoples themselves from travel journals written many years ago.

An interesting literary position on the Polish publishing market is Maciej Kuczyński's novel "Waterfall" (Kuczyński 2010) which is a story about a shamanistic journey. A seriously ill man goes on a last trip to the Amazon rainforest, where his wife works with a native Brazilian group. The main character, Robert, wants to meet her before losing the battle with cancer. In the course of events, the man is healed by the shaman and his own wife, who, however, cannot get out of the trance. At this point, the actual plot begins, because the protagonist must access the supernatural world himself and, with the help of a friendly shaman, defeat the enemy forces in order to bring his wife back to real life. In the foreword, the author emphasizes that "shamanistic threads and practices are based . . . on the reports of anthropologists, especially Michael Harner, as well as on the author's personal contacts with this researcher and other academic researchers" (Kuczyński 2010: 6), which is a strong credibility basis for the events presented later (and also indicates links with neo-shamanism). The narrative incorporates elements of the scientific world as well, as the protagonist's wife is a scientist who specializes in shamanism. This inclusion adds credibility and instills trust in the reader.

Robert visits the Xingu people – a name that appears at the beginning of his journey (Kuczyński 2010: 72) – who actually live along the Xingu River (the states of Pará and Mato Grosso in Brazil). It is not a unified group – it consists of several subgroups, some of which live in Parque Indígena do Xingu (Xingu Native Park) established in 1961 (PIB n.d.2).

The events in the novel are set around a shamanistic journey that Robert must undertake to save his wife. Immersed in the supernatural realm, Robert wields a shaman-crafted stick as his safeguard against malevolent spirits. Various figures of the mythical world appear in the story – diades, elves with pointed ears, giants, fairies, gnomes, and many others – as well as the spirits of animals sent to fight heroes and spiritual beings, and even Venusians with their spaceship (as we learn, as one of the few they can navigate both worlds and can be encountered in reality and in the supernatural world). The world of spiritual beings is presented as a second, parallel world where thoughts and willpower have the power to shape reality (therefore the protagonist can turn into a bird or an anaconda and his physical form is solely a matter of his own imagination and a need arising at a given moment). There are various forces, both good and bad, among which there is a hierarchy of importance and power. Of course, the supernatural world, as the protagonist himself notes, is seen by him in a certain way due to culture and upbringing, so it would probably look different to others. This explains the author's numerous cultural lending (e.g., from Nordic or Slavic myths).

The supernatural world shown in the novel, full of various energies and powers suggestively described by the author, watches over our world. In addition, each of us at the moment of birth prepares all decisions and choices and "inevitably heads towards them" (Kuczyński 2010: 158). This is very far from Amazonian shamanistic practices. The presented practices are actually a mixture of different cultural elements. Examples are *tsentsaki*, or spiritual arrows sent by shamans (Kuczyński 2010: 158), the word *yachay* to describe a shaman of extraordinary power (Kuczyński 2010: 242) or the synonymous use of the words *ayahuasca* and *yagé* – they all come from different cultural practices (in these particular cases *tsentsaki* come from the practice of Shuar shamans in Ecuador and Peru, *yachay* comes from the language of Quichua also in Ecuador, while *ayahuasca* and *yagé* are prepared from the same plant *Banipteriopsis caapi*, but they differ in the way they are processed and in their effect). Such examples could be multiplied, but after reading the introduction to the book, it is not difficult to guess where it came from: since the author based (as he himself emphasizes) on Michael Harner's works and conversations with him, it becomes obvious that neo-shamanistic practices found their way to his prose. Michael Harner dealt with a search for universal elements of shamanism (Harner 1980) and this is reflected in Kuczyński's novel. This can be seen in the use of *ayahuasca* to find the truth about oneself and about the world (the protagonist considers this in terms of "enlightenment", which he experienced by being allowed to access "one of the mysteries of existence" – Kuczyński 2010: 294), in the search for visions, as well as in the universality of the presented shamanic practices. In the text, there is information that shamanism serves the community (Kuczyński 2010: 158), but in the layer of events, the reader learns how neo-shamanism works and what to expect from it.

The supernatural world presented in the book is governed by its own laws, and the protagonist is subjected to constant trials, from which he emerges victoriously thanks to his love for his wife. In the end, the supernatural world turns out to be inhabited by good, wise beings who watch over both sides of the world and look after our fate. It is an interesting vision, because the shamans' accounts indicate that the realm of spiritual beings is perilous and challenging to access, requiring significant effort on their part to navigate.

An element that draws attention in Kuczyński's narrative is the style of the statements of the Indigenous protagonists (both real and spiritual) – a bit fancy and full of "higher knowledge" (e.g., "You, the first of the whites, understood what this treasure meant to us and the Indian tribes and their forest spirits" – Kuczyński 2010: 276 – or "As the King commanded me, I drank the infusion and went into the underworld, like you, white man. But I will stay here, and you will return to your human brothers" – Kuczyński 2010: 210), giving these protagonists a character known from the "Indian" novels of the 20th century. It is almost expected that one of these characters will end his statement with the word *howgh*, based on the model of the story about Winnetou.[1] It should be noted however, that the author presents (neo)shamanistic practices in an interesting way, showing a significant dose of cultural relativism.

The shamanism of *Green Hell* (Creepy Jar 2019) is similarly depicted. In one of the deserted villages, the player encounter a vessel filled with *ayahuasca* and a backpack with slightly burnt notes about its use. One of the choices is to drink a beverage (first you need to collect the leaves needed to finish the infusion), after which the protagonist experiences visions. In the description of the *ayahuasca* ritual presented in the game, you can read that its participants experience a "spiritual revelation", and "wonderful visions show them the purpose and true nature of the cosmos and the reason for their existence", as well as "memories of their past lives" (Creepy Jar 2019: note found by a player during the game). It has little to do with the practices of the Indigenous inhabitants of the Amazon region, but rather with the neo-shamanistic approach. The further part of the description also explains that vomiting and diarrhea are normal reactions of the body after taking *ayahuasca*, which means that the body is purified this way, and this also constitutes one of the neo-shamanistic elements (shamanistic practices are not necessarily associated with sudden reactions of the body), as well as the information that the Indigenous people possessed great memory and concentration thanks to taking *ayahuasca*. Misrepresentation of facts is an indicator of the influence of neo-shamanistic ideas on the popular understanding of shamanism and it finds its reflection in this game.

The search for the truth about oneself and the image of a "Great Mother" is also presented in Alice Walker's novel "Now is the Time To Open Your Heart" (Walker 2004). The author of the book, known primarily for her award-winning "The Color Purple" (Walker 1982), has been active in the area of defending human rights as well as all living beings for many years, so she is always on the side of the oppressed for economic, religious or political reasons (Walker n.d.). Her numerous texts are usually socially engaged – and against this background, the novel "Now is the Time To Open Your Heart" is an exception, because it is a story about a couple who, looking for a separate place in the world, find their way to each other. The story told does not refer to great politics or economy-related matters, but rather to human dilemmas and individual search for freedom. Kate is one of the protagonists. During her journey she goes to the tropical forest and undergoes a multi-day session with the use of *ayahuasca*. To some extent, we are dealing with a mixture of neo-shamanism and the so-called *ayahuasca* tourism, because Kate joins a group led by a shaman (from an ethnic group that is not specified), whose members are looking for "higher knowledge", expecting that it will free them from guilt, bad memories or show the way to a better life. The presented shamanistic practices are mainly limited to taking *ayahuasca*, which is accompanied by violent reactions of the body (up to the general exhaustion appearing after many days of these experiences). The songs of the shaman are also mentioned in a language that none of the newcomers understand ("maybe the language of the Mayans or Quechua. It does not matter" (Walker 2004: 95). This fact already is worrying in the message when it comes to the reliability of presenting spiritual practices). When the protagonist experiences a trance induced by a hallucinogenic agent, the concepts of "Grandmother", "Grandmother spirit" and the animal aspect of each person appear (Walker 2004: 65), because by definition, the experiences of strangers to the Amazonian culture will correspond to what they have learnt about shamanism in the Western culture. This is directly confirmed in the novel in reference to the writings of Carlos Castaneda (Walker 2004: 148, 165). Therefore, we are dealing with neo-shamanism, dressed in more ethnic clothing, because *ayahuasca* is interchangeably called *yage* (Walker 2004: 70) and one of the first visions is always a great anaconda (Walker 2004: 72), and the shaman leading the group sings healing songs called *ícaros* (Walker 2004: 65). The latter are an important element of traditional shamanistic practices in the Amazon region, and come from plants that have "passed their knowledge on to shamans" (Luna 1984). The exchange of information and experiences between man and nature is a part of the acquisition of shamanic knowledge in Amazonian cultures. *Ícaros* are testimonies of the knowledge and power of the shamans, and their role depends on the situation. Some increase or weaken the patient's state of trance, others treat a specific disease or call for help in the form of *spirits* (Luna 1984: 146). Shamanic healing songs come primarily from Peru, but today they can be found in various regions of the Amazon and are practiced by both traditional shamans and so-called *vegetalistas*, that is, Mestizo shamans (Black 2014). Another reference to the culture of the Amazon is the words of the shaman who runs the program in the novel, which states that his clients experience "what people [experienced] thousands of years ago . . . and have been experiencing for thousands of years. *Grandmother Yagé* is the cure for the beginnings and the ends" (Black 2014: 166). The characters of the book enter into a state of trance to heal themselves by accessing the subconscious – they want to release their fears and experiences so that they can start a new life in peace of mind, and this is to happen by "opening the heart" (Walker 2004: 207). Hence, the title of the novel, and this "openness" is to be associated with the understanding of the meaning of nature, human community and the role of every person in the world. Characters undergo a kind of therapy, and (neo) shamanism is only a tool enabling them to overcome internal barriers – probably it is a tool more colorful in the novel than, for example, a psychoanalytic session or group therapy.

The above-mentioned *ícaros* also became the basis of a sound essay in which the sounds of nature mix with the singing of shamans from the Amazon region (in this particular case from the Peruvian region – Narby and Huxley 2004). The artists gathered in the Soundwalk Collective (2012) tried to present the process of taking over the powers of spiritual beings by shamans through learning and repeating melodies specific to them. In a later version, images of the night forest and the faces of shamans intersect – both the sound version and the image added is an artistically processed documentary record of shamanistic practices. On the one hand, this is an interesting approach, but on the other hand, it makes the viewer certain that the image of the inhabitants of the Amazon as people living in "ancient times" is real. Brazilian artists referred to a similar topic in their video installation, in which transparent Indigenous characters were shown on a green background made of fragments of fabrics and video of the forest (Motta and Lima 2008). Thus, people were shown as part of the nature – on their green skin you can see a drawing of leaves and the texture of the fabric.

Note

1 The protagonist of the series of books by Charles May published in German in 1875–1910. In the following years, May's stories were translated into many languages and became the basis for the European image of North American Indigenous people.

References

Allende, I. (2002). *La ciudad de las bestias*. Debolsillo.
Besette, C. (2008). *Yai Wanonabälewä: The Enemy God* [film]. USA. Gospel Communications International. Length: 93 minutes.
Biet, A. (2004). Evoking the Devil: Fasting with Tobacco to Learn How to Cure (1664). [in:] *Shamans Through Time. 500 Years on the Path of Knowledge*, ed. J. Narby. Penguin.
Black, S. (2014). *Ícaros: The Healing Songs of Amazonian Curanderismo and Their Relationship to Jungian Psychology*. https://pdfs.semanticscholar.org/22b6/4e0e25ae4c3ed07dffaf65b91e56899c9397.pdf.
Brown, M.F. (1989). Dark Side of the Shaman. The Traditional Shaman's Art Has Its Perils. *Natural History*, 98(11), 8–10.
Castaneda, C. (1968). *The Teachings of Don Juan: A Yaqui Way of Knowledge*. University of California Press.
Centro Yachak. (2012). https://www.centroyachak.org/2012/09/nacion-shuar.html (accessed 12.08.2019).
Cherry, L., & Plotkin, M. (2001). *The Shaman's Apprentice*. Voyager Books.

Countinho, J.P. et al. (2013). Aspidosperma (Apocynaceae) Plant Cytotoxicity and Activity Towards Malaria Parasites. Part I: Aspidosperma nitidum (Benth) Used as a Remedy to Treat Fever and Malaria in the Amazon. *Memórias do Instituto Oswaldo Cruz*, 108(8), 974–982.
Creepy Jar. (2019). *Green Hell* [video game]. Poland.
Devereux, G. (2004). The Shaman is Mentally Deranged. [in:] *Shamans Through Time. 500 Years on the Path of Knowledge*, ed. J. Narby. Penguin.
Eliade, M. (1974). *Shamanism: Archaic Techniques of Ecstasy*. Princeton University.
Fausto, C. (2004). A Blend of Blood and Tobacco: Shamans and Jaguars among the Parakanã of Eastern Amazonia. [in:] *Darkness and Secrecy. The Anthropology of Assault and Witchcraft in Amazonia*, ed. N. Whitehead, & R. Wright. Duke University Press.
Gow, P. (1996). River People: Shamanism and History in Western Amazonia. [in:] *Shamanism, History and the State*, ed. N. Thomas, & C. Humprey. The University of Michigan Press.
Guerra, C. (2015). *El Abrazo de la Serpiente (Embrace of the Serpent)* [film]. Colombia. Ciudad Lunar Producciones. Length: 125 minutes.
Harner, M. (1980). *The Way of the Shaman. A Guide to Power and Healing*. Harper&Row.
Hussey, C. (2005). *The Valley of Secrets*. Hodder Children's Books.
Kenin-Lopsan Mongush, B. (1997). *Shamanic Songs and Myths of Tuva*. Akademiai Kiado.
Kopenawa, D., & Albert, B. (2013). *The Falling Sky: Words of a Yanomami Shaman* (N. Elliot, trans.). Harvard University Press.
Kuczyński, M. (2010). *Wodospad* [waterfall]. Wydawnictwo SOL.
Luna, L.E. (1984). The Concept of Plants as Teachers Among Four Mestizo Shamans of Iquitos, Northeastern Peru. *Journal of Ethnopharmacology*, 11(2), 135–156.
Motta, G., & Lima, L. (2008). *Amoahiki (Shamanic Song Trees)* [video installation]. CCBB Rio de Janeiro.
Narby, J., & Huxley, F. (eds.). (2004). *Shamans Through Time: 500 Years on the Path to Knowledge*. Tarcher/Penguin.
Navarro, B. (2012a). [Online video]. https://www.youtube.com/watch?v=mKxxmcpxJmU&t=111s&ab_channel=BarbaraCraneNavarro.
Navarro, B. (2012b). *The Way of the Shaman* [performance].
Navarro, B. (2014). *YANONAMI Film for Children* [short film]. USA. N/A. Length: N/A.
Neumann Fridman, E.J. (2004). *Sacred Geography: Shamanism Among the Buddhist Peoples of Russia*. Academiai Kiado.
Overing Kaplan, J. (1981). Amazonian Anthropology. Review Article. *Journal of Latin America Studies*, 13, 151–164.
Oviedo, G.F. (2004). Devil Worship: Consuming Tobacco to Receive Messages from Nature (1535). [in:] *Shamans Through Time. 500 Years on the Path of Knowledge*, ed. J. Narby. Penguin.
PIB. (n.d.2). https://pib.socioambiental.org.br/en/Povo:Xingu (accessed 02.02.2024).
Platt, R., & van Wyk, R. (2004). *The Vanishing Rainforest*. Frances Lincoln Children's Books.

Plotkin, M.J. (1993). *Tales of a Shaman's Apprentice: An Ethnobotanist Searches for New Medicines in the Amazon Rain Forest*. Penguin Books.
PluggedIn. (n.d.). https://www.pluggedin.com/movie-reviews/yaiwanonablew theenemygod (accessed 24.02.2024).
Ramos, A. (1995). *Sanumá Memories: Yanomami Ethnography in Times of Crisis*. The University of Wisconsin Press.
Roe, P. (1982). *Comic Zygote: Cosmology in the Amazon Basin*. Rutgers University Press.
Rollins, J. (2002). *Amazonia*. William Morrow.
Sieroszewski, W. (1935). *Dwanaście lat w kraju Jakutów, cz. II*. Instytut Wydawniczy "Bibljoteka Polska".
Soundwalk Collective. (2012). *Ayahuasqueros. Radio France Culture*. J. Narby (dir.) [Online]. http://soundwalkcollective.com/radio-commissions/.
Tantra. (n.d.). https://www.tantra.pl/szamanizm/warsztaty-szamanskie/; http://dompodlipa.pl/warsztaty-szamanskie-moc-jednosc/ (accessed 24.02.2024).
Thevet, A. (2004). Ministers of the Devil Who Learn About the Secrets of Nature (1557). [in:] *Shamans Through Time. 500 Years on the Path of Knowledge*, ed. J. Narby. Penguin.
Virtanen, P.K. (2015). Fatal Substances: Apuriña Dangers, Movements and Kinship. *Indiana*, 32, 85–103.
Vitebsky, P. (1996). *Szaman* (Dalewski Z., trans.). Muza S.A.
Walker, A. (1982). *The Color Purple*. Harcourt.
Walker, A. (2004). *Now is the Time to Open Your Heart*. Phoenix.
Walker, A. (n.d.). https://alicewalkersgarden.com/about/ (accessed 27.02.2024).
Wallis, R. (2003). *Shamans/Neoshamans: Ecstasy, Alternative Archaeology, and Contemporary Pagans*. Routledge.
Walsh, R. (2010). *The World of Shamanism: New Views of an Ancient Tradition*. Llewellyn Publications.
Walter, M.N., & Neumann Fridman, E.J. (1994). *Shamanism. An Encyclopedia of World Beliefs, Practices, and Culture* (Vol. 1). ABC Clio.
Whitehead, N., & Wright, R. (eds.). (2004). *In Darkness and Secrecy. The Anthropology of Assault and Witchcraft in Amazonia*. Duke University Press.
Whitten, N.E. (1976). *Sacha Runa: Ethnicity and Adaptation of Ecuadorian Jungle Quichua*. University of Illinois Press.
Whitten, N.E. Jr. (ed.). (2003). *Millennial Ecuador*. University of Iowa Press.
Wierucka, A. (2015). *Huaorani of the Western Snippet*. Palgrave.
Wierucka, A. (2018). Living with Strangers: Huaorani and the Tourism Industry in the 21st Century. *Anthropological Notebooks*, 24, 97–110.
Yost, J. (2010). https://vimeo.com/5102150 (accessed 24.02.2024).
Znamenski, A.A. (2007). *The Beauty of the Primitive: Shamanism and Western Imagination*. Oxford University Press.

Cannibalism

An intriguing cultural element that captures popular imagination about the Amazon is undoubtedly cannibalism – in the colloquial sense, it stands in contrast to European humanism, recognizing the inherent value of humanity. The term "cannibalism" appeared during Christopher Columbus's second voyage to the Caribbean Islands in 1493, where the inhabitants of the Antilles were identified as consuming human flesh. Later, this term was used in descriptions of other groups, not limited to South America (Lindenbaum 2004: 477). As mentioned earlier, the first accounts of Amazonian inhabitants emphasized cannibalistic practices. Amerigo Vespucci, in his account from 1503, described, among other cultural practices, the cannibalism of the encountered Indigenous people (Vespucci 1894: 47).

Similar descriptions were provided by Hans Staden in his work published in 1557, where he detailed the Brazilian Tupinamba group and their custom of eating human flesh (Staden 1557). Subsequent centuries systematically built an image of cannibalistic practices. As Waldemar Kuligowski (2007) writes, one of the significant sources contributing to this portrayal was excerpts from the work of Jesuits published in a single volume in the late 18th century (Jesuits 1780). The monks described various customs of Indigenous people (in this case, inhabitants of North America), emphasizing elements inconsistent with their own cultural norms, including alleged cannibalism. Such revelations stem from the denial of the "foreigner's" belonging to the world of human norms – typically, it involved deviations from European cultural principles. It was also claimed that the consumption of human flesh was practiced on all continents except Europe, leading to the hierarchization of societies and even questioning the humanity of those who engaged in such practices (Kuligowski 2007: 4). In effect, however, accounts of cannibalism say more about those who wrote them than about those they described (Kuligowski 2007: 11).

Among the Amazon Basin groups, ritual cannibalism, according to William Arens' classification, took two forms: endocannibalism (consumption of the body – usually ashes – of a deceased relative) and exocannibalism (consumption of the body of someone outside the group, often an enemy – Arens 2010: 47). Ritual cannibalism was governed by many rules and did not involve eating people in the same way as regular food. In recent years, the best-known example is the practices of the Wari' group in western Brazil – consuming the body of a deceased relative was an expression of sympathy for the deceased person and their family (Conklin 2001: xvi). The expectation was to consume the entire body, and sometimes even the bones of the deceased (Conklin 1995: 75). Wari' believed that not eating even a tiny bit would harm the memory of the deceased and the dignity of their family. Several months after the funeral ritual, the shaman told the deceased's family that he had appeared as a peccary (*Tayassu pecari*), seen as evidence that the deceased person had fully integrated into the community of ancestors. The peccary, in turn, became food for relatives, representing the only way to have a nonviolent interaction between the ancestor and the living individuals (Conklin 2001: 205).

Ritual cannibalism is also practiced in other Amazonian groups, including the Chapakuran, Aché-Guayaki, and those belonging to the Panoan linguistic group, as well as the Yanomami, who consume the ashes of deceased relatives (Jacob n.d.). According to Beth Conklin, Amazonian endocannibalism aims to remove the body to sever the relationships between the body and the spirit of the deceased and between the living and the spirits of the dead (Conklin 2001: xxviii). It was also a crucial aspect in the formation of social relations and identity (Conklin 1995: 76).

Exocannibalism is much rarer, and in the Amazon, it is practically only associated with the Wari', who practiced it before contact with the Western world, until the late 1950s. Eating the bodies of people outside the group was linked to warlike actions – parts of the bodies of defeated enemies were roasted and eaten, expressing hatred and hostility, deeming the enemy as subhuman, symbolically equating their body with animal meat (Vilaça 1992: 47). Between 1956 and 1969, the Wari' gradually ceased both forms of cannibalism, a direct result of their contact with the external world (Conklin 1997: 70). Other groups also practiced exocannibalism in the past – such as the Tupinambá, Guarani, Chiriguano (until the 16th–17th centuries), and Shipaya and Juruna (until the 19th century – Fausto 2007: 508). However, the "rediscovery" of exocannibalism in the mid-20th century in the case of the Wari' and the reaction of the Western world associated with it reinstated the stereotype of the "Amazonian cannibal".

Carlos Fausto argues for a different perspective: Amazonian residents pay much attention to spiritual and bodily transformation, believing that all beings in the cosmos potentially can be humans. In this understanding, transformation manifests in an overlapping cycle where a human becomes "non-human" matter and vice versa (Fausto 2007: 501). Peter Gow adds that peccaries (which, for many groups, appear as transformed ancestors) are eaten not only to satisfy hunger but also to create kinship bonds (Gow 2001: 70). In this context, the consumption of human flesh appears as a factor creating relations between people and between what is human and what is "non-human" or "super-human".

Shaping the image of Amazonian Indigenous people 75

The cannibalism stereotype played a significant role in colonial politics – it provided a basis for exterminatory actions because Indigenous people were considered inferior or even subhuman (Conklin 1997: 68). Cannibalism provided the strongest weapon for European control (Conklin 1997: 69), the effects of which are still visible today.

A good example of stereotypical thinking about the Amazonian peoples as cannibals can be found in film productions. Many horror films set in the Amazon in the 20th century were based on this stereotype (such as "Jungle Holocaust" – Deodato in 1977, "Cannibal Apocalypse" – Margheriti in 1980, or "Emmanualle and the Last Cannibal" – D'Amato 1977), and the 21st century has not spared its viewers from more productions on this topic.

In recent years, one of the titles in this genre is "Green Inferno" (Roth 2013). The title itself is interesting, as it is neither the Spanish "inferno verde" nor the English "green hell", but a combination of both language versions, which, in fact, is not specifically justified in the content of the film. The plot of the film is relatively simple: a group of committed American students decides to save the rainforest by attaching themselves to trees and stopping bulldozers from destroying the environment where the "last isolated people in the world" live. Deforestation is the first step in the illegal activities of a gas-extracting company – the subsequent steps, as described by the characters, involve destroying the village and killing its inhabitants. After the students crash their plane, they end up in the village they intended to save and now become the food because, of course, the Indigenous people are cannibals. There is no place for ritualistic cannibalism – the successive Americans are dismembered with machetes, roasted in a clay oven, and then consumed by the villagers. The first victim is essentially eaten alive: before the man dies and is roasted, his eyes and tongue are gouged out, his hands and legs are severed. The scene of sprinkling salt on the man's corpse and placing a fruit resembling an apple in the mouth of the severed head is completely absurd (a typically Euro-American approach to "roasting"). These are not the only elements that provoke objection, not because of the display of violence but because of the lack of logic.

About the group (called Yajes – it's not hard to guess that it doesn't exist), we learn very little from the film: all the inhabitants are painted red, their hair is cut somewhat resembling the Yanomami, they walk almost naked, and live in huts covered with palm leaves. In the community, two people stand out in appearance – a shaman and a shamaness, or chief and shamaness (it's hard to determine because, apart from their leadership position and some fear shown to them by the other group members, we don't learn anything more). Their appearance resembles the shamans of New Guinea (the shaman has a body painted black and yellow, with animal fangs protruding from his nose; the shamaness wears long robes, has bead strings stretched from nose to ears, uses a bone staff adorned with a human shoulder blade, and a large animal claw for various harmful actions against newcomers, etc.), and at the same time, they do not represent any spirituality. The group, referred to in the film as the "last isolated" raises pigs and cows, which is usually one of the first effects of contact (new economy is imposed on the local people, which, from the authorities' point of view, is more suitable for modern times). Group members wear decorations made of sticks on their faces, which again resembles the Yanomami – this is dangerous due to the difficult contemporary situation of this group because associating them with cannibals can seriously harm their reputation in Venezuela and Brazil, where over 20,000 Yanomami still live. Returning to the group's image in the film: all its members are basically portrayed as mindless people, waiting only for the next meal and blindly obedient to their leaders. The main heroine manages to escape from the village with the help of a boy who is the only one showing any human feelings – they lead him to cut the girl's bonds at the last moment before her death (truth be told, we do not know what the villagers wanted to do with her, because in this one case, they discover that she has her period and ceremonially paint her, then tie her up, and the shamaness intends to perform an unspecified ritual on her, which the girl manages to avoid).

The cannibalistic practices shown in the film fall into the horror category, to which this position is assigned: there are bloody human bodies and severed heads impaled on stakes in the village, the body is cut with a machete, and all the inhabitants eagerly consume the roasted flesh of their victims. The only elements that in any other way depict everyday life are baskets and clay dishes, but this is too little to build any cultural framework, so the Indigenous people appear as powerless beings driven by the lust for cannibalism.

Anthropophagic elements can also be found in the film "Yai Wanonabälewä: The Enemy God" (Besette 2008), but it is portrayed without sensationalism, as a normal cultural practice. The presentation of the custom does not sensationalize violence, and if the main character did not comment on this fact, the viewer might not realize the meaning of the scene. The description of cannibalism in Isabel Allende's (2002) novel is similar – after the death of the chief, his remains are burned, and the ashes mixed with food are eaten by all the inhabitants of the village as a gesture of respect for the chief.

In many cultural texts I have analyzed, mentions of various forms of cannibalism appear, but they are usually marginal and not exaggerated (as an example, in the film "The Lost City of Z" [Gray 2016], Europeans, upon reaching the village of Indigenous people, are shocked by the sight of human skulls lying in ashes and a human body still hanging over the hearth – they declare that they have arrived at a group of cannibals. However, Fawcett explains to them that through this practice, the Indigenous people eat the spiritual essence of deceased group members).

References

Allende, I. (2002). *La ciudad de las bestias*. Debolsillo.
Arens, W. (2010). *Mit ludożercy. Antropologia i antropofagia* (W. Pesse, trans.). Wydawnictwo Uniwersytetu Warszawskiego.

Besette, C. (2008). *Yai Wanonabälewä: The Enemy God* [film]. USA. Gospel Communications International. Length: 93 minutes.
Conklin, B. (1995). "Thus are Our Bodies, thus was Our Custom": Mortuary Cannibalism in an Amazonian Society. *American Ethnologist*, 22(1), 75–101.
Conklin, B. (1997). Consuming Images: Representations of Cannibalism on the Amazonian Frontier. *Anthropological Quaterly*, 70(2), 68–78.
Conklin, B. (2001). *Consuming Grief: Compassionate Cannibalism in an Amazonian Society*. University of Texas Press.
D'Amato, J. (1977). *Emmanuelle and the Last Cannibal* [film]. Italy. Length: 99 minutes.
Deodato, R. (1977). *Jungle Holocaust* [film]. Italy. Length: 92 minutes.
Fausto, C. (2007). Feasting on People: Eating Animals and Humans. *Current Anthropology*, 48(4), 497–530.
Gow, P. (2001). *An Amazonian Myth and Its History*. Oxford University Press.
Gray, J. (2016). *The Lost City of Z* [film]. USA. Amazon Studios. Length: 141 minutes.
Jacob, F. (n.d.). They Eat Your Ash to Save Your Soul: Yanomami Death Culture. https://www.academia.edu/3632663/They_Eat_Your_Ash_to_Save_Your_Soul_Yanomami_Death_Culture (accessed 20.11.2023).
Jesuits. (1780). Lettres édifiantes et curieuses éctrites des missions étrangeres. *Mémoires du Levan*, Chez J.G. Merigot. https://archive.org/details/lettres-difiant04jesu/page/n7/mode/2up (accessed 31.01.2024).
Kuligowski, W. (2007). *Antropologia współczesności. Wiele światów, jedno miejsce*. Universitas.
Lindenbaum, S. (2004). Thinking About Cannibalism. *Annual Review of Anthropology*, 33, 475–498.
Margheriti, A. (1980). *Cannibal Apocalypse* [film]. Italy. Length: 96 minutes.
Roth, E. (2013). *Green Inferno* [film]. USA-Chile. Blumhouse Productions. Length: 100 minutes.
Staden, H. (1557). *Warhaftige Historia und beschreibung eyner Landtschafft der Wilden Nacketen, Grimmigen Menschfresser-Leuthen in der Newenwelt America gelegen*. https://archive.org/details/staden/page/n1/mode/2up (dostęp 31.01.2024).
Vespucci, A. (1894). *The Letters of Amerigo Vespucci and Other Documents Illustrative of His Career* (C.R. Markham, trans.). Burt Franklin.
Vilaça, A. (1992). *Comendo como gente: Formas de canibalismo Wari*. Editora UFJR.

Contemporary issues

The problems that Indigenous inhabitants of the Amazon currently face include industrialization, the influx of tourists, political issues, and matters related to identity. Many groups no longer speak their native languages and do not continue traditions. To some extent, it is not surprising, as they live in the 21st century, often in cities or in close contact with them, using modern technology just like other residents of these regions. Therefore, it is unlikely that they would plan their lives the same way as their grandparents. However, it seems possible to maintain traditions and the Indigenous way of life in the modern world. For example, some young people from certain Huaorani groups in eastern Ecuador would prefer to live like their ancestors (Wierucka 2021). Of course, this applies only to certain aspects of life, such as living in a forest village, hunting, cultivating gardens, or practicing shamanism, as these youths also have access to electricity, mobile phones, and the internet.

A growing problem is tourism. People from other continents come to the Amazon to see untouched nature and experience contact with Indigenous groups. Tourists who want to see (and often primarily photograph) Indigenous people of a particular region visit local villages, markets, and other places. The worst situations occur when visitors treat local residents as objects in a zoo – observing, taking photos (often without permission), and behaving inappropriately. There are, of course, tactful tourists who leave a positive impression and do not cause harm to the culture, but warnings have been issued that tourism poses a threat to local residents due to their exoticization (Martinez-Gugerli 2019). As Kristen Martinez-Gugerli writes, tourists expect people in the Amazon and their culture to be unchanged remnants of what once was. This expectation reflects the visitors' mindset. As John Urry wrote, to some extent, local residents become part of the environment and are perceived as its elements (Urry 1992: 4).

In anthropology, there is an ongoing debate about the impact of tourism on the cultural practices of Indigenous groups (e.g., Greenwood 2004; Ness 2003; Reid 2003; Wallace 2005), and this issue also extends to the Amazon, where tourists expect to encounter a "mysterious forest inhabited by timeless, environmentally friendly indigenous people" (Hutchins 2007: 79).

Tourists' expectations are also exploited by local agencies providing various types of tourist services. Indigenous people of the Amazon are often presented in their countries for tourism purposes as "primitive", "living like their ancestors", or "the last true" Indigenous people (Wierucka 2018). Local people become suitable for advertisement when portrayed as nearly naked, representing a certain level of "primitiveness" (Hutchins 2007: 79).

Tourism also has a flip side – often, groups that perceive tourism as an option for economic stabilization (which is not easy to achieve in this region of the world) transform cultural and historical elements to attract tourists (Babb 2012: 47). As a result, tourists receive what they expect, while local residents ensure a steady income. This creates a closed loop of demand and supply, where the visitor sees what has been specially prepared for them. Interestingly, the untrained eye of the tourist cannot distinguish between what originates from the local culture and what has been added to enhance the experience.

In the meantime, the term "ethnotourism" (tribal tourism) has emerged, in which tourists not only visit specific Indigenous groups but actively participate in their cultural life (Oakes 2000: 204). However, even this type of practice often does not show the true face of the life of a particular group but rather a staged version. Research indicates that ethnotourism brings more harm than benefit; for example, rituals turn into performances, groups not interested in contact are forced into it due to their "attractiveness" to tourists (e.g., the case of the Mashco-Piro group in Peru – Kranstover 2014), biodiversity disappears, and overall, the cultural costs are too high (e.g., youth no longer want to speak their native language). The proposed solution is responsible tourism, where participants are educated about cultural and economic issues, ensuring that their money goes directly to the host group.

The daily problems faced by Indigenous inhabitants of the Amazon are usually not represented in artistic cultural texts. If they are, it is in a marginal form. The theme that reaches the awareness of the Western world through cultural texts is industrialization and the deforestation it causes. Many works for children, such as "The Vanishing Rainforest" (Platt and van Wyk 2004) mentioned earlier, address this issue. Indigenous people know that if the forest disappears, animals, their main source of food, will vanish, as will local medicinal plants (Platt and van Wyk 2004: 21). Tourism is often seen as remedy for this situation. Communities decide to build cabins for tourists, and the income is planned to be used for education, healthcare, and "for the government to keep *nabë* [strangers] farmers away" (Platt and Wyk 2004: 24). It is not the best solution for the reasons I described earlier – tourism does not provide a cost-free way out for a given cultural group and often causes more harm than benefit. However, in this context, it is presented as a solution to deforestation problems, internal group issues, and as a way to preserve identity.

Sometimes, topics important to the local residents of the Amazon appear in cultural texts in the background of other events, serving as a backdrop for the actions of protagonists, often those arriving in the tropical forest for a different purpose. One such situation occurs in the previously mentioned Harlequin series book (Wicks 2018), where a doctor and a nurse travel to the Amazon as part of medical volunteering. Before their journey to the Amazon, the protagonists discuss the location of their planned activities on the border of Brazil, Venezuela, and Guyana and the group living there: the Ingariko. This is the actual name of the people living near Mount Roraima – the Ingarikó, as mentioned before. The doctor in the novel travels to this group to assist in medical treatment, but the Indigenous thread completely fades away in the narrative because it is not the focus of the author's interest (and likely not of the readers who expect something different from this type of literature). In the burgeoning romance between the doctor and the nurse, there exists an opportunity to address the issue of limited access to healthcare and education for Indigenous communities, alongside challenges stemming from drug trafficking and gold mining. This latter problem also appears in some films, such as "Welcome to the Jungle" (Berg 2013), where the characters fight with the landowner who owns a gold mine. In the Amazon, gold is mainly found in riverbeds and is washed by the water – gold prospectors, using mercury compounds and lemon juice, work to combine gold particles into larger nuggets visible to the naked eye. However, in the discussed film, the search for gold is shown spectacularly, as it refers to the Serra Pelada mine in Brazil. Gold was discovered there in 1979, and in the 1980s, tens of thousands of people arrived in hopes of quick enrichment. Photos from the mine show the dramatic conditions in which they worked – images circulated of thousands of people climbing ladders, carrying bags of soil on their shoulders, and digging soil in search of gold nuggets (Rare Historical Photos n.d.). Individuals engaged in the extraction of gold-bearing soil did so willingly, driven by the aspiration to attain wealth. However, in the film "Welcome to the Jungle", they are portrayed as enslaved residents of the town under the control of the mine owner. Of course, the film ends with their liberation and the elimination of the bandits, which certainly does not always happen in Brazilian conditions. Still, the film at least addresses the significant issue for the Amazon, which is the plundering extraction of natural resources.

Interestingly, one video game, "Green Hell" (Creepy Jar 2019), also addresses the topic of illegal gold mining in the Amazon. The notes received by the player contain information about areas that were previously enveloped in lush green vegetation and now constitute empty, toxic wastelands poisoned with mercury. The comments of the characters presented in the game speak of the "destruction for the price of gold", indicating the commitment of the game's authors to contemporary problems in the Amazon, even though only verbal commentary on this topic is presented during the game. Similarly, in a conversation between characters – a translator and an anthropologist who later embarks on a solitary search for a partner in the forest – there is information about a book written by an anthropologist that brought "media, scientists, and doctors to the local tribe, and the World Health Alliance set up a medical camp and probably conducted studies beyond the tribe's taboo". This short fragment might refer to the research conducted on the Yanomami by American researchers, who, among other things, took blood samples, which was inconsistent with local customs. Napoleon Chagnon and James Neel, during their research among the Yanomami, took their blood for testing but did not receive proper permission. As Gabriel Elizondo writes, Chagnon misled the Yanomami by telling them that the blood samples would be used for their benefit, while they were actually used for research (Elizondo n.d.). After several years, when the researched individuals from the Indigenous community passed away, the blood samples were returned to the Yanomami group and they were ritually buried (Survival International 2015). The echo of these events can definitely be found in information about the Yabahuaca group presented in the game.

Gold mining is also referenced by Isabel Allende (2002) in her novel. Additionally, characters discuss the construction of roads through pristine forest regions, neglecting the well-being of local inhabitants and displacing them to more isolated areas. There are also mentions of the military failing to uphold their duty of protecting the Indigenous peoples, and the smuggling of protected animal species – it is a rare case in cultural texts to present not only historical but also contemporary problems. Charmian Hussey's novel (2005) falls into both of these categories. As mentioned earlier, events in the book take place in two periods – at the beginning of the 20th century and in the vaguely defined present because the grandson of one of the characters reads a travel journal from the Amazon and learns about slavery during the rubber collection period and other crimes of that time (Hussey 2005: 240). The ancestor of the young protagonist meets someone in the Amazon resembling Roger Casement, who is investigating the abuses of the rubber industry against local residents. However, the information seems improbable to him at the time. News of genocide is unacceptable to Europeans traveling through Brazil, and it seems exaggerated to them (Hussey 2005: 240). Soon, however, they find out the truth: the group in which they lived for a year, which became their family, was abducted, and all its members were killed by the "rubber barons". The grandson of the travelers obtains this information at the end of the 20th century, and his conclusion is one: not much has really changed over these hundred years because "today's barons of the Amazon forest are beef barons" (Hussey 2005: 283). The disappearance of successive cultural practices is seen as the "impoverishment of humanity", not only of individual people but also of

> the knowledge of an ancient culture . . . – songs and dances; myths and legends; the wealth of knowledge about the forest; plant lore and herbal medicine – knowledge acquired over thousands of years, all wiped out with the people themselves.
>
> (Hussey 2005: 418)

The author also finds a place for comments on groups remaining in voluntary isolation and the destructive construction of roads, attempts at contact against the will of local people, or flooding Indigenous areas by building dams. All these problems indeed affect the Indigenous inhabitants of the Amazon, and their placement in the novel seems extremely valuable in this regard. Similar themes are addressed in the film "Amazon Forever" (Dutilleux 2004) in which a young filmmaker goes to the Kamaiurá village and eventually becomes involved in the protection of the rainforest. The documentary he produces is intended not to document cultural practices but to show how illegal logging destroys the rainforest. The young Frenchman strives to raise awareness among Europeans, yet the film illustrates the immense challenge inherent in this endeavor: the majority of people are apathetic toward such matters. It is regrettable that the discussion of these issues is comparatively infrequent when compared to other topics in literature and media.

The case of the drama "Amazônia" (Teevan and Heritage 2008) is intriguing in this context, as it portrays the return of the spirit of Chico Mendes to advocate for the preservation of the local rainforest in Brazil. Francisco Alves Mendes Filho, known as Chico Mendes, was a rubber tapper and activist who, in the 1980s, was the first to publicly call for the reduction or complete cessation of tropical rainforest logging. He argued that it leads to soil infertility, erosion, and river pollution. Mendes became a pioneer and symbol of a new environmental protection system involving the creation of reserves by local residents responsible for their care (EDF 2020). Mendes' work also inspired new environmental protection laws in Brazil (WWF 2018). His death in 1988 at the hands of cattle ranchers echoed worldwide and influenced awareness of environmental protection (BBC 2020a). In the drama "Amazônia", Mendes returns as a defender of the forest, explaining to local residents that selling wood from the cleared forest won't enrich them: "But the earth, the earth here is not fertile without the trees. In a few years this land will be a wasteland" (Teevan and Heritage 2008, act 1, scene 8). The villagers are convinced by a young economist that selling wood is the only way out of poverty, and they collectively cut down the forest. In the end, when everyone understands the consequences, Mendes advises the solution: "Look after your own community, your own forests, your own parks and your own rivers. Fight for them and encourage those people with whom you live and love to protect your traditions, to preserve your environment and to care for your people" (Teevan and Heritage 2008, act 2, scene 6). The drama's message is ultimately positive and, while didactic, encapsulates in simple words what is most important for local environmental actions.

The drama "Amazônia" was staged in 2008 at the Young Vic Theatre in London, but the critics did not positively evaluate the performance, considering that the simple story of saving the rainforest, intended to raise awareness of its value, was lost in an overly elaborate production (colorful costumes, spraying the audience with water in the river scene, clowns, etc. – Fisher

2008). The play was directed by one of the co-authors of the text, Paul Heritage, which makes such treatment of the story even more surprising.

The film, which straddles the border between what could be called local, Amazonian creativity and a product of Euro-American culture, is "La terra degli uomini rossi" (Bechis 2008) directed by Marco Bechis, born in Brazil and residing in Italy, which undoubtedly influences the tone of the film. The main roles are played by Guarani people, most of whom had their first contact with acting. Unlike many other discussed cultural texts, this film is essentially a manifesto for changing the situation of the Guarani-Kaiowá in the Mato Grosso do Sul region of Brazil. The lands belonging to this group were taken from them many years ago, and currently, Indigenous people occupy small pieces of land from which it is impossible to make a living (Survival International n.d.3). The traditionally owned areas have been completely transformed into plantations and pastures of new owners. Guarani consistently try to occupy even small areas of their former lands, which usually ends in violence from plantation workers, the military, and the police (Survival International n.d.3). The story told in Bechis' film begins with the suicide of two Guarani-Kaiowá teenagers, as a result of which their family decides to leave the reserve village and occupy a piece of land near the plantation of a Brazilian owner. The story is reminiscent of the true story of Marcos Veron, whose fate was similar to that of the leader of the group shown in the film: for his unwavering stance and peaceful return to the ancestors' land in 2003, he was murdered by plantation workers (Branford 2003). Bechis' film thus addresses the most significant problems related to the life of Brazil's Indigenous peoples: the increase in suicides (especially among young people), the lack of prospects, the loss of tradition, and violence from authorities and society. The Indigenous people in this film are portrayed contemporarily, naturally, without exoticization, and cultural practices are not sensationalized but shown as an integral part of their life. The film was produced in collaboration with Survival International, an organization dedicated to the rights of Indigenous groups, so the depicted image intentionally differentiates it from other cultural texts. At the end of the film, additional information is shown: before year 1500, about 5 million local residents lived in what is now Brazil, and today only a small number remains, still affected by ethnocide (Bechis 2008, 01:33:34). While the events presented are fictional, very similar ones often occur, and Indigenous people struggle with daily life as well as corruption, violence, misinterpreted laws, and human unfriendliness. The last frame of the film is a symbolic, never-ending field completely devoid of forest, with one lone tree growing on it – symbolically picturing what remains of the vast Amazon rainforest and its inhabitants.

Another depiction of contemporary problems of Brazil's Indigenous peoples is found in the short animation "Pajerama" (Cadaval 2008), and despite being somewhat local, originating from the Amazon, the vision of local people does not differ much from the popular one. A Yanomami boy during a hunt in the forest is surprised by various elements of Western technology, starting from a subway stop sign and ending with a big road running through a city of glass skyscrapers. Afterward, the hunter returns to the forest and goes to an older Yanomami man. At the moment they sit together, a subway stop sign appears right in front of them – all the experiences of the young man turn out to be a prophecy of what will happen in his tropical rainforest. The film is visually beautiful, the scenes are well supported by music, and a few minutes of the film keep the audience in suspense. The film talks about what is probably inevitable: the Western world will intrude into the tropical rainforest with its technology, and it probably won't leave much behind – evidence of this can already be seen today.

The artist Barbara Navarro, who addresses current issues in Brazil, also deals with contemporary and historical descriptions of the problems of Indigenous Amazon residents in her performance titled "The Forest is Burning" (Navarro 2012b). Symbolically outdoors, she burned vertically hanging strips of fabric representing a tree trunk. In one of the performance photos, a streak of fire from the burning installation is led to a characteristic basket woven by the Yanomami. The message is clear: when the Amazon forests burn, the cultures existing there will also perish because the forest is their support in every respect – economic, social, and ideological. The performance's progress can be seen in a film where the burning act is enriched with sounds and images from the Yanomami village (Navarro 2012a).

The series "Frontera Verde" (Guerra 2019) also addresses the contemporary and historical descriptions of the problems faced by local residents, with the action taking place in two periods, the present day and almost 80 years earlier. The difficulties faced by local residents are the same: illegal logging, murders of those defending the forest, corruption, diseases transmitted by outsiders, etc. Indigenous people are powerless against these threats, and this situation has not changed over the past century, as the series vividly shows. Only the ways of seizing forest resources and the speed at which it happens have changed.

In the previously mentioned film "Amazon Forever" (Dutilleux 2004), one of the Brazilian characters comments, providing a good summary of the contemporary problems concerning Indigenous groups: "We still have people starving in our country. Food, education, basic medical care – these are our national priorities, not protecting Indians or the rainforest. That is the luxury of rich countries" (Dutilleux 2004, 01:14:15).

References

Allende, I. (2002). *La ciudad de las bestias*. Debolsillo.
Babb, F.E. (2012). Theorizing Gender, Race and Cultural Tourism in Latin America. *Latin American Perspectives*, 39(6), 36–50.
BBC. (2020a). https://www.bbc.com/news/av/stories-51021984 (accessed 22.02.2024).

Bechis, M. (2008). *La terra degli uomini rossi (Birdwatchers)* [film]. Brazil. Lilt Films. Length: 104 minutes.
Berg, P. (2013). *Welcome to the Jungle* [film]. USA. Universal Pictures. Length: 95 minutes.
Branford, S. (2003). Chef Marcos Veron (Obituary). *The Guardian*, 28 January. https://www.theguardian.com/news/2003/jan/28/guardianobituaries (accessed 22.02.2024).
Cadaval, L. (2008). *Pajerama* [short animation]. Brazil. N/A. Length: N/A.
Creepy Jar. (2019). *Green Hell*. Polska.
Dutilleux, J.P. (2004). *Amazon Forever* [film]. France. N/A. Length: N/A.
EDF. (2020). *Enviromental Defense Fund*. https://www.edf.org/chico-mendes-living-legacy (dostęp 06.02.2024).
Elizondo, G. (n.d.). *Bitter Fight Over Brazilian Blood: Why the Yanomami Tribe Want Blood Samples Taken by the US Scientist Back*. http://anthroniche.com/darkness_documents/0547.htm (accesses 20.02.2024).
Fisher, P. (2008). https://www.britishtheatreguide.info/reviews/YVamazonia-rev (accessed 22.02.2024).
Greenwood, D.J. (2004). Culture by the Pound: An Anthropological Perspective on Tourism as Cultural Commodity. [in:] *Hosts and Guests. The Anthropology of Tourism*, ed. V.L. Smith. University of Pennsylvania Press, pp. 169–186.
Guerra, C. (2019). *Green Frontier: Limited Series (Behind the Scenes)*. Netflix.
Hussey, C. (2005). *The Valley of Secrets*. Hodder Children's Books.
Hutchins, F. (2007). Footprints in the Forest: Ecotourism and Altered Meanings in Ecuador's Upper Amazon. *Journal of Latin American and Caribbean Anthropology*, 12(1), 75–103.
Kranstover, G. (2014, July 22). *Deteriorating Cultures: The Destructive Effects of Tribal Tourism*. Council on Hemispheric Affairs. http://www.coha.org/deteriorating-cultures-the-destructive-effects-of-tribal-tourism/
Martinez-Gugerli, K. (2019, April 15). *How Ethnotourism Exoticizes Latin America's Indigenous Peoples* [panoramas]. Scholarly Platform.
Navarro, B. (2012a). [Online video]. https://www.youtube.com/watch?v=mKxxmcpxJmU&t=111s&ab_channel=BarbaraCraneNavarro.
Navarro, B. (2012b). *The Forest is Burning* [performance]. http://www.barbaranavarro.com/Performance-The-Forest-is-Burning.
Ness, S.A. (2003). *Where Asia Smiles: An Ethnography of Philippine Tourism*. University of Pennsylvania Press.
Oakes, T. (2000). Ethnic Tourism. [in:] *Encyclopedia of Tourism*, ed. J. Jafari. Routledge.
Platt, R., & van Wyk, R. (2004). *The Vanishing Rainforest*. Frances Lincoln Children's Books.
Rare Historical Photos. (n.d.). https://rarehistoricalphotos.com/hell-serra-pelada-1980s (accessed 22.02.2024).
Reid, D.G. (2003). *Tourism, Globalization and Development: Responsible Tourism Planning*. Pluto Press.
Survival International. (2015). https://www.survivalinternational.org/news/10727 (accessed 22.02.2024).
Survival International. (n.d.3). https://www.survivalinternational.org/tribes/guarani (accessed 22.02.2024).

Teevan, C., & Heritage, P. (2008). *Amazônia*. Oberon Books.
Urry, J. (1992). The Tourist Gaze and the Environment. *Theory, Culture, Society*, 9(1), 1–26.
Wallace, T. (2005). Tourism, Tourists and Anthropologists at Work. *NAPA Bulletin*, 23(1), 1–26.
Wicks, B. (2018). *Tempted by Her Hot-Shot Doc*. Harlequin Mills & Boon Limited.
Wierucka, A. (2018). Living with Strangers: Huaorani and the Tourism Industry in the 21st Century. *Anthropological Notebooks*, 24, 97–110.
Wierucka, A. (2021). Negotiating Better Futures: Migration of Huaorani Youth in Rural Ecuador. *Journal of Youth Studies*, 25(3), 307–320. https://doi.org/10.1080/13676261.2020.1869195.
WWF. (2018). *World Wildlife Fund*. https://www.wwf.org.br/?69202/30-years-with-Chico-Mendes (accessed 22.02.2024).

4 The tropical forest as a living environment

All stories about the Indigenous peoples of the Amazon, to some extent, also speak about the tropical forest, which forms the foundation of the life and culture of its inhabitants. Sometimes the forest serves as a character equally as important as the people involved in the described events, while other times it simply serves as a backdrop – however, in both cases the creators (with few exceptions) usually follow certain conceptual or imaginary stereotypes. Of course, the manner in which the tropical forest was depicted and understood changed over time, however it did not affect its use in literature, film or other arts today.

The tropical forest includes the richest ecosystems and the greatest biodiversity in the world. It is often understood as the "wildest" and most "natural" (as opposed to "cultural") place in the world. Betty Meggers in her text dated 1954 defined the tropical forest as a constraint on the development of cultures – in her opinion, the environmental conditions of the forest allowed for only a certain manner of development (Meggers 1954). At the same time, the forest was presented as eternal, primordial, and timeless. Later archaeological discoveries changed the understanding of the forest – there were opinions about the "anthropogenic forest", meaning one that constitutes the result of human activity for centuries (Balée 2006: 75–90). The forest found by visitors from Europe was not something "timeless" in this sense – it was shaped by the people living there. Meggers' proposal was therefore rejected and historical ecology emerged as a science discussing the mutual impact of the environment and people in ancient times. Indigenous peoples sowed seeds, planted trees, cultivated clusters of native forests, took advantage of vegetation for generations (Rival 2016: 84–88), but, as Nicholas Kawa points out, the concept of "anthropogenic forest" places too much emphasis on human activity, and too little on the existence of the forest as such (Kawa 2016: 98), full of plants, animals, and even bacteria or parasites, because they all affect its condition and vitality. If man has had an impact on it in past millennia, it is not in its entirety. Posthumanists propose a different approach, in which man does not constitute the center of attention, but becomes only an element of a larger whole (Ferrando 2016: 18). Eduardo Kohn undertook "anthropology beyond

DOI: 10.4324/9781003495055-4

humanity" (Kohn 2013: 7) seeking meanings beyond what is human and what also represents the world (Kohn 2013: 8). Therefore, man is not the only being (in this case, in the tropical forest) who understands the world – traditional Indigenous knowledge does not distinguish between culture and nature in the same way as in the Western thinking that comes from the Judeo-Christian tradition. Moreover, the environment undergoes constant changes and man is not the only being responsible for this transformation (Kawa 2016: 108).

The tropical forest is a complex system functioning in delicate balance. It can be called "a mature ecosystem that achieved stability allowing for quickly processing dead matter and its reintegration into the living system. It does not include surplus of nutrients or mineral banks to use when the system is disrupted" (Forsyth and Miyata 1984: 19). In this type of environment, there is no accumulation of humus or deepening of the soil layer – in fact, the tropical forest grows on weak, shallow soil, and the essence of its vitality is the continuous rotation of organic matter.

The Indigenous communities residing in the Amazon perceive the forest in a manner distinct from representatives of Western culture who analyze the forest plants through the lens of Linnaean taxonomy. Meanwhile, the Indigenous people understand the forest as a complex system in which everything is dependent on each other. For example, the Huaorani people from eastern Ecuador call each part of the plant differently depending on the degree of its maturity. No plant exists as a separate entity – it always constitutes a part of a network of interconnected organisms such as plants, insects, birds, and other animals (Davis 1996: 276–277). A plant constitutes rather a representative of its species, "treated as an individual member of a class belonging to a specific environment, and as a specific living organism undergoing a continuous process of change" (Rival 2016: 86). This means that for local residents, the forest is a living, constantly changing, complex organism. Moreover, it is understood as a part of everyday life, as well as a source of spirituality. For example, for the Shuar group, living in the forest means

> being absorbed in a world where humans and non-humans walk, jump, fly, and crawl . . ., the sunlight and the dark of the night which provide the conditions for life in a jungle where to live means interaction and socialization between human and non-human spheres.
> (Abad Espinoza 2009: 156–157)

Moreover, for the Shuar people, the heavenly and earthly worlds are connected by a symbolic liana, so all beings of these spheres are connected and communicate with each other (Abad Espinoza 2009: 178). In this context, the activity of colonizers, and later the administrations of individual countries located in the Amazon, seem to be an over-exploitation not only in terms of destroying the forest, but also the entire ecosystem as well as the basis of Indigenous beliefs and cultural practices. The local people also interfered with the tropical forest, but they preserved biodiversity and did not lead to its destruction. What the first European migrants called a "forest" often constituted mixed groves planted by the natives (Smith 1999: 139), but during the period of colonization, when the Indigenous people could not take care of their lands, these places were absorbed by the surrounding vegetation. However, to this day, in many cases, clusters of, for example, Peach palm (*Bactris gasipaes*) located in the forest, are treated as a trace of ancestors living in a given location (Rival 2016: 54). Therefore, the forest has not only economic but also cultural significance and is a very important element in the life of Indigenous groups in this region. This situation changed in the 16th century, after the arrival of the Europeans.

From the very beginning of the conquest and later colonization, the tropical forest was used in an ill-considered manner – no attention was paid to the damage done, because the profit from its resources was most important. Human activity has led to profound changes in the natural environment of the Amazon. Up to the 1970s the tropical forest covered up two-thirds of the Amazon (Goulding et al. 2003: 19), but since then, more than 20% of the forest has been modified, and since the 1980s, more and more information about deforestation appeared. Three issues were of particular concern: reducing the amount of oxygen on a planetary scale, increasing the production of carbon dioxide, and destroying biodiversity (Goulding et al. 2003: 19). Today it is known that tropical forests cannot be treated as the "lungs of the Earth" because the decomposition of vegetation in the Amazon region consumes almost as much oxygen as is produced by living plants, and moreover, oxygen in the atmosphere also comes from other sources not related to the Amazon (e.g., marine phytoplankton – Goulding et al. 2003: 19). However, other doubts concerning the impact of economic development on the tropical forest quickly found their justification in the progressive degradation of the natural environment.

Deforestation constitutes the first step to any other activity – road construction, oil, gas or other natural resources extraction. Today, terms such as "deforestation" and "tropical forest degradation" are distinguished. The first term applies when the forest is irretrievably lost, and the second when its structure and application change (the term "afforestation" is still used, which consists in increasing the area of the forest as a result of human activity and "reforestation" occurring in the case of cutting down the forest and planting a new one on its place, therefore maintaining the forest area in an unchanged size – Lanly 2003). The stage following cutting down trees in the industrialization of the Amazon forests was caused by the aforementioned discovery of rubber vulcanization by Charles Goodyear in 1839 (Plotkin 1993: 179), which led to the over-exploitation of the Brazilian rubber tree (*Hevea brasiliensis*). Large deposits of gold have also been discovered in the Amazon – they have been washed out of the Amazon river waters since the 17th century, but the real "gold rush" took place in the middle of the 20th century, when it was

90 *The tropical forest as a living environment*

possible to reach previously inaccessible areas thanks to the construction of roads. To extract pure gold from the ore, hydrocyanic acid salt is also used, the use of which was supposed to be carefully controlled, but there are known cases of this strong poison leaking into the environment. Today, gold is still mined in the Amazon – for example, in gold mines in Peru, the functioning of which lead to completely depriving the area of any vegetation. Despite the fact that most of these mines are illegal, the Peruvian government has not been able to effectively counteract this for years (Kann 2019; Taj 2019; Carranza 2019).

The tropical forest is also a place of oil and gas extraction – since the 1960s, oil companies have been intensively extracting these raw materials, but because these were companies from outside South America, all profits went to foreign hands. Most oil fields are located in the western part of the Amazon – in Ecuador and Peru (Finer et al. 2008: 2), and some also in Colombia and Brazil. Extracting crude oil is dangerous for the environment mainly due to petroleum waste entering water and soil. It wasn't until 1991 that this case saw the light of day, when Judith Kimerling published a book (1991) revealing the scale of the devastation of the Ecuadorian tropical forest. Since then, actions are carried out not only to clean up the environment, but also to introduce strict rules for oil extraction. A large step toward the expected changes was a judgment issued in 2011 ordering Chevron-Texaco to pay $9 billion in compensation and to repair the damage done to the environment (Romero and Krauss 2011) – unfortunately, the oil company is refusing to comply with this judgment (Chevron n.d.).

Today, only 45% of the Amazon is covered with the primeval forest. The following 46% are subject to economic activities, and 9% have been lost (probably irretrievably) to agriculture, urbanization, etc. (Romero and Krauss 2011). The largest forest conservation project to date consists in the Amazon Region Protected Areas (ARPA), launched in 2002 in Brazil, which aims to convert 600,000 km² of forest into a site of strict conservation and sustainable development (WWF 2014).

Most areas in the Amazon that are still covered by primary tropical forests are located within Indigenous territories granted by the governments of respective nations – in Brazil alone, they account for more than a million square kilometers of land thus protected from destruction (Schwartzman and Zimmerman 2005: 722). The Amazonian countries have also established national parks whose task is to protect the pristine forest, but individual authorities do not always comply with the laws they have passed – a well-known example is the Ecuadorian Yasuní National Park, where, despite numerous protests, oil extraction began in 2013 (Watts 2018). After a decade of activism aimed at preserving the national park, in 2023, the Ecuadorian nation made a historic decision during the referendum to protect the pristine forest and halt all oil drilling in the area (Collyns 2023).

The tropical forest is used in many ways, none of which takes into account losses in the environment and in the culture of the people living there. And yet, "the evolutionary development of the rainforest will never be repeated. . . . Its deconstruction, cattle ranch by cattle ranch, and hydroelectric project by hydroelectric project causes so many cataclysmic changes so quickly on microscopic to a global scales that we can't keep up with its effects" (London and Kelly 2007: 48). If nothing changes in this regard, the refuge of biodiversity, fresh water, and resistance to climate change will be lost (Conservation n.d.).

Information about the tropical forest enchants Europeans – today the same way as over the centuries. In his expedition report, Christopher Columbus described

> groves of lofty and flourishing trees are abundant, as also large lakes, surrounded and overhung by the foliage, in a most enchanting manner. Everything looked as green as in April in Andalusia. The melody of the birds was so exquisite that one was never willing to part from the spot, and the flocks of parrots obscured the heavens. . . . A thousand different sorts of trees, with their fruit were to be met with, and of a wonderfully delicious odor.
> (Columbus n.d.)

Columbus came to the conclusion that the fresh water in the Paria Bay came from the rivers of Eden, described in the Bible (Nawrocka 2010: 31). Since the very beginning, the Amazon was identified as paradise on earth, emphasizing the richness of its nature and the innocence of the people living there.

Las Casas focusing on the injustices concerning the Indigenous peoples witnessed in 16th century, also mentions "a very happy land, where there were vast and delightful lands, valleys forty miles long, very beautiful surroundings" (de las Casas, B. 1992 [1542]: 99). In 1639, a Spanish Jesuit, Cristóbal de Acuña, accompanied Pedro Teixeira from Portugal during a long expedition from Quito to Belem. We owe detailed descriptions of nature to the Jesuit, but also admiration for the richness of the environment and comparisons to a paradise land abundant in all natural goods (de Acuña 2010 [1641]).

Later descriptions also define the Amazon forest in this manner – in 1859, after years spent in the Amazon, the aforementioned Henry Bates said goodbye to the "equator where the well-balanced forces of Nature maintained a land-surface and climate that seemed to be typical of mundane order and beauty", he left "endless streams" and "boundless forests", to finally admit that he spent those years in earthly Eden (Bates 1892).

As noted by Ewa Nawrocka, there is a relation between learning about America and the development of utopian thought in Europe at that time – the New World was presented as a land of happiness and abundance, and its vision was based on the works of Theocritus, Virgil, or sixteenth-century shepherd's novels (Nawrocka 2010: 37).

However, a different vision of the Amazon slowly began to emerge. In 1908, Alberto Rangel published his collection of short stories titled *Inferno verde* ("Green Hell", Rangel 1920), in which he conveyed his views with a quote from the drama of William Shakespeare, already on the title page:

> All torment, trouble, wonder and amazement
> Inhabits here.
> (Shakespeare 2004, act V, scene 1)

Euclides da Cunha, a Brazilian writer, wrote an introduction for Rangel's text, stating that "the Amazon is the last page of the Book of Genesis that has not yet been written" (da Cunha 2001: 27). Cunha traveled through the Amazon and, above all, drew attention to its over-exploitation, which Rangel also describes in his stories. "Green Hell" also stands for the inaccessibility of the environment and the climate: "the Amazon remains locked in an inglorious, endless battle with humans" – obviously for a newcomer from Europe, because the locals have been and are adapted to this climate. Euclides da Cunha later, in 1909, wrote his own essays about the Amazon, published in one volume (da Cunha 2006), in which he admires, among others, the tropical forest already at the very beginning: "during the silent middays (the nights are fantastically noisy), one who might walk the forest does so with their gaze exhausted by the green-black of the foliage and, repeatedly encountering the arborescent ferns, which rival palm trees in height and trees with straight, almost bare trunks, does so with a disquieting sense that they have returned to a much earlier time" (da Cunha 2006: 4).

In 1924, José Rivera's novel "La Vorágine" was published (Rivera 1924), depicting events during the rubber boom. In the novel, the tropical forest is portrayed as a "green hell" where everything poses a threat – lianas are linked by a deadly embrace, there is an abundance of insects and larvae everywhere, as well as much greater threats like diseases, animals, and all this exists in a green labyrinth without a way out. At the same time, the novel also includes a delight over the forest, which is like

> a cathedral where unknown gods whisper endless liturgies, promising the majestic trees, ancient as the Garden of Eden that they will surely live forever. . . . Unyielding as a cosmic force, you [the forest] are the mystery of creation.
> (Rivera 1924: 122)

In the subsequent years of the 20th century, numerous texts – both scientific and popular – were written that maintained this dual portrayal of the Amazon: either as an earthly paradise or as a hell. These representations remain relevant today.

From an early age, we teach children to understand the tropical forest as a paradise space. The most popular children's books that depict the forest "paradise on earth" constitute a part of early school learning – an example of this is the probably most widely known English-language book about the tropical forest from the 20th century, "The Great Kapok Tree", written by Lynne Cherry (2000). It is the story of a lumberjack who has to cut down a kapok tree (*Ceiba pentandra*), one of the largest in the tropical forest. Before work, the lumberjack takes a nap and in his dream he is visited by various animals that whisper into his ear how important the tree he intends to cut down is for their survival. The last to visit him is a boy from a group living in the forest who asks the man for a different look at the nature around him. After waking up, the lumberjack goes away and leaves the tree intact.

The book tells the story of just one tree, but it has the potential to change readers' thinking, as it presents the intricacies of relationships within the tropical forest environment in a simple way. This book is part of the curriculum in grades 1–3 in the United States and influences attitudes toward nature and deforestation. It also allows young readers to understand the effects of deforestation and the necessity of leaving the forest in its natural state for the survival of animals and humans. Interestingly, the portrayal of the kapok tree is not insignificant here – besides being one of the largest trees in the Amazon, it is also home to many plant and animal species. Moreover, it is important for the forest inhabitants: Indigenous peoples used its seeds, leaves, and resin to treat diarrhea, fever, and asthma, and they also attributed special significance to it in their mythology, as it was believed to be inhabited by spiritual beings (Ortiz 2007). Therefore, the choice of this particular tree as the main topic of the book seems all the more justified.

A similar tone is found in the early 21st-century book "The Forest Grew All Around" (Mitchell and McLennan 2007). The story of the forest is presented in the form of a rhyming tale that expands with each page. We follow the journey of a seed that falls to the ground at the beginning of the rhyme, while various animals and plants living in different parts of the tree are introduced. At the end of the book, there are also classroom or home activities, as well as a recipe for "tropical forest cookies" (named because some ingredients come from the forest, such as cinnamon). The forest in this work is teeming with animals, mysterious, and colorful. The descriptions do not explicitly show the relationships between plants and animals, and the tropical forest itself appears self-sustaining and beautiful. The tree depicted here is also the *Ceiba pentandra*.

Undoubtedly, the most famous series of children's books is one by Dr. Seuss, which includes a book about the tropical forest (Worth 2003). The beloved character Cat in the Hat guides two children through the rainforest and tells (in his usual amusing rhyming style) about its different layers inhabited by various plants and animals. The Cat also highlights relationships between different organisms and warns against deforestation (ultimately appealing to loggers to leave the trees alone). The book also includes a glossary of more challenging terms, suggestions for further reading on the rainforest theme, and an index of animals that can be encountered in the forest.

Similar to previous children's works, the forest is portrayed as fascinating, beautiful, and somewhat mysterious.

Children's literature reinforces the image of the tropical forest as a magical place, which is not surprising – no one expects young readers to be presented with the concept of the "green hell". Books "Diário de Pilar na Amazónia" (da Silva 2011) and "Śnieżek and Węgielek" (Snowflake and Charcoal – Wechterowicz 2012) explore the adventures of the young travelers to the Amazon. These adventurers introduce children to the tropical forest and the animals living within it, and additionally, Śnieżek and Węgielek (a white cat and a black dog) engage children in various graphic activities that also impart knowledge (e.g., children are asked to draw patterns on the jaguar's fur or color the snake and butterflies, but first they must learn how these creatures look in nature). Pilar's story includes, for instance, a mermaid living in an Amazonian river, which adds to the magical nature of the place. However, detailed descriptions of plants and animals unique to this area (such as the *Ceiba pentandra* – kapok tree, *Bradypus infuscatus* – sloth, or *Eunectes murinus* – anaconda) are presented in frames on many pages, undoubtedly enhancing the educational value of the book (da Silva 2011: 74, 91, 95).

Similar depictions of the forest can also be found on other children's toys: Granna's "Dzika Amazonia" (Wild Amazon) puzzle (Granna 2014) invokes the extraordinary forest with its name alone, and the assembled picture features colorful plants and numerous animals (from jaguars and snakes to frogs, spiders, and mosquitoes), all depicted in vibrant colors and full of life. Meanwhile, Anna Sobich-Kamińska's board game "Odkrywcy. Amazonia" (Explorers: Amazon – Sobich-Kamińska 2017) encourages young players to discover the "beautiful tropical forests and amazing animals". During the game, players can learn about animals characteristic in this region, including some completely unknown to Europeans (such as the *Didelphis marsupialis* – black-eared opossum, *Dendrobates tinctorius* – blue poison dart frog, or *Cebuella pygmaea* – pygmy marmoset). However, on the back of the game board, only the names of the animals featured in the game are provided, lacking additional information about the Amazon ecosystem and the depicted animals. The game takes the form of an expanded domino set, which is an interesting proposition, especially as it is beautifully illustrated by Ewa Geruzel, but it leaves a certain feeling of dissatisfaction.

In Isabel Allende's book (2002), the forest is both beautiful and dangerous – initially, the travelers seeking the titular "beast" are enthralled by the forest and its "paradisiacal" appearance, with descriptions of a "magnificent green cathedral" of trees inhabited by colorful birds and unique animals found nowhere else. However, they soon realize that the forest is also perilous not only because predators roam within it but also because it makes one feel extremely isolated and incapable of coping with nature – as emphasized by the characters, survival is only possible with the help of Indigenous people (Allende 2002: 63). A similar depiction appears in other novels, including those by Eva Ibbotson (2014) and Katherine Rundell (2017): the tropical forest in them is enchantingly beautiful yet not devoid of threats. Ibbotson's protagonist, upon returning to England, responds to her friends' inquiry about what it's like to be rescued by saying she was probably rescued from paradise (Ibbotson 2014: 284). For her and her fellow travelers, the Amazonian forest is a place they belong to (Ibbotson 2014: 249), and they eventually manage to return there. On the other hand, in Rundell's novel (2017), four children lost in the tropical forest discover its beauty and strive to survive, ultimately returning to their families in Europe. The young heroes learn about nature, realizing that what seemed to be just greenery is actually composed of thousands of shades of green.

A similar portrayal of the forest is found in the Netflix series "Frontera Verde" (Guerra 2019b): the shots depict it as an immeasurable green expanse or a tangled thicket. In subsequent episodes, the audience learns that the forest is also magical, with its immortal guardians, and that it is one big organism where everything depends on each other. The forest is a living entity that communicates with chosen individuals, assigns them tasks, and relies on their care. All of this is shown through excellent aerial shots and close-ups. The stunning footage of the Amazon forest and rivers adds significance to this series – the creators of the series have made the forest a separate character in the narrative not only because it has the ability to communicate with humans but primarily because it has its own personality, power, and decision-making ability. The producers of the series emphasize that even during production, it became apparent that they had to "communicate with nature because it holds the power here" (Guerra 2019a, 00:4:35). At the same time, the intention was to maintain the "mystery of the forest" and portray it as powerful, impenetrable, and even dark (Guerra 2019a, 4:59).

In most movies and novels, the forest is portrayed rather as a challenging place to live and full of dangers. An example could be the book "The Amazon Code" (Thacker 2016), in which travelers navigate through "the densest forest they've ever seen", which becomes "a foreign world" because it is so far removed from what they could have expected (Thacker 2016: 190). One of the characters even states that the rainforest

> doesn't have to be more mystical or magical than any other place. Sure, there is more life per square foot here than anywhere on the planet, but that's all it is: life. . . . Not everything wants to kill you, and even those lifeforms that can, will only do so if they feel their own is threatened.
> (Thacker 2016: 190)

At the same time, descriptions of the forest and its inhabitants are full of colors and sounds, so the picture that emerges from them rather opts for a "paradisiacal garden" than a "green hell", although the journey of the heroes is not devoid of threats from nature.

The tropical forest has also become a good backdrop for video survival games – the aforementioned Polish game from 2019 (Creepy Jar 2019b) already in its title "Green Hell" refers to the portrayal of the forest as a dangerous and difficult place to master. During gameplay, the player must learn how to survive in these unusual conditions, especially since they are attacked by various animals (as well as warriors from one of the local groups, who in this case are portrayed as part of nature, a component of the forest), and nature constantly sets new traps. As the game's creators describe it, it is a simulator of "survival in an open, explorable, unique environment of the Amazon rainforest. . . . The game tries to faithfully reflect the conditions prevailing in the Amazon jungle" (Creepy Jar 2019a). And indeed, the portrayal of the tropical forest is faithful, perhaps except for moments when there is more space and bare rocks, which hardly occur in the forest. However, it is also shown as a source of food and medicine, which the player-character learns during the gameplay. At the same time, the tropical forest seems boundless and full of mysteries.

A similar portrayal can be seen in contemporary films – even the horror film "The Green Inferno" (Roth 2013) shows the forest as an endless green space, and the nature in the film looks very natural. For the untrained Euro-American eye, "everything is the same" (Roth 2013, 0:42:36), which makes the characters unable to find their way in the forest.

In the previously discussed thriller novel "Amazonia" by James Rollins (2002), the forest also plays an intriguing role – it is dangerous, almost deadly for outsiders, and at the same time, it is an ideal place to carry out the action described in the book. At the beginning, the described forest is presented as a "vast sea of green – spread to the horizon" (Rollins 2002: 79) and the protagonists arriving there for the first time discover that "the understory of the Amazon rain forest was not a clotted mass of clinging vines and overgrown vegetation. Instead, it was more like they were marching through a green cathedral" (Rollins 2002: 88), and as events unfold, they also learn about the medicinal properties of the plants growing in it (Rollins 2002: 125) and their extraordinary adaptations to natural conditions: for example, there is a paragraph about *Triplaris americana* (referred to colloquially as the "ant tree" in the book – Rollins 2002: 217), known for the symbiosis of the tree and the ants living in it (the tree provides them with its interior for a colony and sweet nectar as food, while the ants defend it against other animals and plants – CABI 2017).

However, the novel predominantly features the description of an impassable tropical forest, full of unexplored places, which serves as the backdrop for a fantastic tale of a lost world. The valley into which the travelers arrive seems frozen in time – and in a distant time at that, as the scientists among the group describe it as having formed during the existence of Pangaea. The tree they encounter is said to come from a time before the species *Homo sapiens* existed; the valley is full of representatives of long-extinct plant species, such as giant cycads and primitive conifers or ferns (Rollins 2002: 323). Along the way to the valley, the forest depicted in the novel becomes increasingly dangerous – the travelers are attacked by extraordinary, bloodthirsty creatures that do not belong to any known species. As one can easily guess, they are a product of the valley, as the ancient tree growing in it is a kind of "ant tree" – it makes plants and animals (including humans) dependent on itself. It provides them with the valley to live in, its trunk, and sap, which has miraculous regenerative properties, but at the same time, it does not allow them to leave the valley because depriving the organism of the ability to constantly consume the healing sap leads to rapid degeneration of the organism and death. As one of the characters explains, because the tree "wants to keep its privacy. If someone flees, anyone the escapee encounters would sicken and die, leaving the trail of death" (Rollins 2002: 424). This is achieved through "prions", which, once introduced into the organism, must be constantly neutralized by successive doses of sap from the tree – if this does not happen, the prion rebuilds and attacks the host causing disease (Rollins 2002: 424). Furthermore, the tree "collects" the genetic patterns of various creatures in caves among its gigantic roots, doing so by storing individual specimens of each species (including humans, such as the father of one of the characters they set out to find). The fantastic nature of this novel is only emphasized by the fact that the tropical forest was the perfect setting for a story about an ancient tree that weaves its own plans regarding the species existing on Earth. The forest is depicted as an extraordinary place, full of possibilities that we cannot foresee.

A similar approach was used by Nick Thacker in his thriller novel (2016) – the valley into which the characters arrive is an extraordinary tectonic creation, unseen in that part of the world. It could have been placed in the Amazon due to its location described as being far from any known part of that area. Again, similar to Rollins' "Amazonia" (2002), in Thacker's thriller "The Amazon Code" (2016), there are plants with extraordinary, almost magical properties – this time it is a tree bearing yellow fruits that enable communication among the inhabitants without words, creating a shared realm of thought. The tropical forest appears as a miraculous place full of extraordinary possibilities. Similarly, in Ann Patchett's novel (2011), in an undisclosed location in the Brazilian Amazon, a certain species of tree grants the local inhabitants the ability to bear children until old age. The "miraculous" tree grows only in one fairy-tale-like place, where "there was no thick coat of undergrowth covering the ground, just a light wash of grass, there were no hairy ropes strangling the trees, only a smooth, straight expanse of bark. Sunlight fell easily between the pale oval leaves and hit the ground in wide patches" (Patchett 2011: 257). The trees, whose bark provided people with extraordinary life options, coexisted with fungi and moths, and "there has been no evidence that this ecosystem is duplicated anywhere else in the rainforest, anywhere in the world" (Patchett 2011: 258). A plant growing in the one and only place in the world (i.e., the Amazon) also appears in Jessica Khoury's novel (2012) – in this case, it is about flowers whose nectar provides immortality. The unexplored spaces of the tropical forest allow for the weaving of even the most improbable stories – such an image contributes to understanding the Amazon forests as a miraculous place where anything is possible.

A similar depiction of the forest is presented in Charmian Hussey's novel (2005) – in her work, the tropical forest is a miraculous source of herbal medicines and a place full of extraordinary animals. The characters bring an endemic species of animals in several variations to Europe, and soon – due to the advancing deforestation and destruction of the Amazon – this group of animals becomes the only one to survive, living in secrecy on the estate of former travelers in Cornwall. Through the mouths of her characters, the author expresses sorrow and incomprehension at the ongoing degradation of the tropical forest. The young protagonist learns that nature is ruthlessly destroyed in the name of progress and decides to change something about it in the near future. The difference he notices between the beginning and the end of the 20th century in the state of the Amazon forests is so striking that it's hard for him to believe, realizing that if the destruction is not stopped soon, the tropical forest will disappear from the face of the Earth (Hussey 2005: 420).

A different portrayal of the forest is presented in film "Jungle" (McLean 2017), based on the biographical book by Yossi Ghinsberg, recounting his getting lost for 20 days in the tropical forest in 1981 (Ghinsberg 2006). The events depicted show the main character's struggle for life in the Amazon, where he is threatened not only by nature (wild animals, parasites, or the density of the forest) but also by his own weakness. Ghinsberg manages to survive because he is found by one of the surviving companions on the journey.

In the film, there are descriptions related to the forest (e.g., "This is the last frontier on Earth, still alive, still wild" – McLean 2017, 00:15:36), but the imagery speaks for itself: the travelers navigate through the forest, float down the river, and nature proves to be untamed. The forest is mysterious, fascinating, and relentless for those from outside the Amazon. It's not Eden, but definitely a "green hell" from which one must escape. In this film, the forest is one of the two main characters – Ghinsberg struggles with it day by day, stubbornly refusing to give up. While there are some inaccuracies in the forest depicted in the film (e.g., the main character marvels at a morpho butterfly at night – *Morpho sp.* – which is a daytime butterfly), the dangers of the forest and its variability are portrayed very realistically. Similarly, in the film "Embrace of the Serpent" (Guerra 2015), which – although shot in black and white – excellently captures the richness of the forest traversed by travelers.

The Amazon rainforest also appears in many films and books where it serves solely as a backdrop – its purpose is to create horror, mystery, and also threats directly related to the presence of unknown animals and plants. An example of such use of the forest can be seen in the film "Welcome to the Jungle" (Berg 2013), where an ambitious bodyguard is tasked with finding and bringing his employer's son back home from the Amazon. During the journey of the two main characters through the forest, they encounter, for example, predatory baboons attacking them (which do not actually exist in the Amazon) or dangerous plants. The terrain they traverse is surprisingly mountainous – it looks like the wooded Andes, which is not surprising when we check the location of this production: Puerto Rico. It has little to do with the Amazon forest, but certainly allows the director to showcase spectacular falls along steep slopes.

In popular literature, the Amazon rainforest also appears as a backdrop – essentially, events could take place elsewhere, but the Amazon adds a more mysterious – or romantic – dimension to them. In the Harlequin series mentioned before (Wicks 2018), for example, the romance develops independently of the location, although the Amazon adds a dose of excitement and unexpected possibilities.

Similarly, in computer games, the tropical forest serves as the setting for actions taken by the characters and poses a threat to them. For example, in "Shadow of the Tomb Raider" (an adventure in the Peruvian jungle – Crystal Dynamics 2018), the protagonist must contend with obstacles encountered in the forest to fulfill her mission, but the environment she finds herself in is only a backdrop for her actions. Additionally, in the Amazon forest depicted in the game, there are structures resembling Mayan buildings from Central America, as well as "Quechua monoliths", which obviously have no place there (the name only corresponds to an Indigenous group inhabiting Peru), as the inhabitants of the Amazon did not build with stone. A similar method of "discovering" ancient stone structures resembling Mayan cities in the tropical forest of the Amazon was used in Katherine Rundell's novel (2017). However, the forest is portrayed realistically.

There are also games that use the term "tropical forest", but it is not presented as an actual forest – this is the case in "Civilization VI" (Firaxis Games 2016) when resources are used in the Brazilian Amazon to build cities and develop civilization. You can also build Chichen Itza, one of the most famous Mayan structures still existing today on the Yucatan Peninsula in Mexico, which has nothing to do with the Amazon. Players on forums also share advice on forest clearance: it is not worth cutting down too much because later in the game when you still have resources, you can quickly use them to win – so the signal players receive is as follows: it's not worth caring for or preserving the forest because later in the game, it can be used for faster "civilization" development (Fandom 1 n.d.) (although you can establish national parks in the game, they must be possible to be occupied by the player, so completely inaccessible areas – e.g., mountains – cannot become parks – Fandom 2 n.d.). The game in this case has little to do with the actual tropical forest and its inhabitants – Brazilian civilization is treated as a development option in a forested area that can be freely modified, and although the forest itself is described as "dark, intrusive, impassable, and deadly" (Fandom 3 n.d.), it is not very evident in the game.

Therefore, the Amazon rainforest is used as a paradise on earth, a hell, or an unexplored place that holds incredible possibilities, such as miraculous plants or animals. This portrayal of the rainforest, initiated at the beginning of colonization, continues to this day, although circumstances and technology have changed.

References

Abad Espinoza, L.G. (2009). A Moral Philosophy of Nature: Spiritual Amazonian Conceptualizations of the Environment. *Open Journal of Humanities*, (1), 149–190.
Allende, I. (2002). *La ciudad de las bestias*. Debolsillo.
Balée, W. (2006). The Research Program of Historical Ecology. *Annual Review of Anthropology*, 35, 75–98.
Bates, H. (1892). The Naturalist on the River Amazons. *D. Appleton*. https://www.gutenberg.org/cache/epub/2440/pg2440-images.html (accessed 22.02.2024).
Berg, P. (2013). *Welcome to the Jungle* [film]. USA. Universal Pictures. Length: 95 minutes.
CABI. (2017). *Digital Library*. https://www.cabi.org/isc/datasheet/119848#tosummaryOfInvasiveness (accessed 22.02.2024).
Carranza C. (2019, March 11). Peru Running Out of Ideas to Stop Illegal Mining in Madre del Dios. *In-Sight Crime*. https://www.insightcrime.org/news/brief/peru-illegal-gold-mining/ (accessed 12.11.2013).
Cherry, L. (2000). *The Great Kapok Tree*. Voyager Books.
Chevron. (n.d.). *Chevron Oil Company*. http://www.chevron.com/ecuador/ (accessed 20.02.2024).
Collyns, D. (2023). Ecuadorians Vote to Halt Oil Drilling in Biodiverse Amazonian National Park. *The Guardian*, 21 August. https://www.theguardian.com/world/2023/aug/21/ecuador-votes-to-halt-oil-drilling-in-amazonian-biodiversity-hotspot (accessed 22.02.2023).
Columbus, C. (n.d.). *Extracts from Journal*, 21 October. https://sourcebooks.fordham.edu/source/columbus1.asp.
Conservation. (n.d.). https://www.conservation.org/places/amazonia (accessed 22.02.2024).
Creepy Jar. (2019a). https://creepyjar.com/gry/ (accessed 22.02.2024).
Creepy Jar. (2019b). *Green Hell* [video game].
Crystal Dynamics. (2018). *Shadow of the Tomb Raider. Peruvian Jungle* [video game].
da Cunha, E. (2001). Preâmbulo. [in:] *Inferno Verde*, ed. A. Rangel. Canas e Cenarios do Amazonas, Editora Valer.
da Cunha, E. (2006). *The Amazon: Land Without History* (R. Sousa, trans.). Oxford University Press. (first issue in Portuguese titled À margem da história, published in 1909).
da Silva, F.L. (2011). *Diário de Pilar na Amazónia*. Jorge Zahar Editor Ltd.
Davis, W. (1996). *One River: Explorations and Discoveries in the Amazon Rainforest*. Simon & Shuster.

de Acuña, C. (2010 [1641]). *Voyages and Discoveries in South-America the First Up the River of Amazons to Quito in Peru, and Back again to Brazil, Perform'd at the Command of the King of Spain by Christopher D'Acugna: The Second Up the River of Plata, and Thence by Land to the Mines of Potosi by Mons Acarete: The Third from Cayenne into Guiana, in Search of the Lake of Parima, Reputed the Richest Place in the World* (M. Grillet, trans.). Printed for S. Buckley. https://quod.lib.umich.edu/e/eebo/A65182.0001.001/1:1?rgn=div1;view=fulltext (accessed 2.12.2023).

de las Casas, B. (1992 [1542]). *A Short Account of the Destruction of the Indies.* Penguin Books.

Fandom 1. (n.d.). https://civilization.fandom.com/wiki/Brazilian_(Civ6) (dostęp 09.09.2019).

Fandom 2. (n.d.). https://civilization.fandom.com/wiki/National_Park_(Civ6) (dostęp 09.09.2019).

Fandom 3. (n.d.). https://civilization.fandom.com/wiki/Rainforest_(Civ6) (dostęp 09.09.2019).

Ferrando, F. (2016). Posthumanizm, transhumanizm, antyhumanizm, metahumanizm oraz nowy materializm. *Różnice i relacje. Rocznik Lubuski*, 42(2), 13–26.

Finer, M., Jenkins, C.N., Pimm, S.L., Keane, B., & Ross, C. (2008). Oil and Gas Projects in Western Amazon. Threat to Wilderness, Biodiversity and Indigenous Peoples. *PLoS One*, 8.

Firaxis Games. (2016). *Civilization VI* [video game].

Forsyth, A., & Miyata, K. (1984). *Tropical Nature: Life and Death in the Rain Forests of Central and South America.* Simon & Shuster.

Ghinsberg, Y. (2006). *Jungle: A Harrowing True Story of Survival.* Boomerang New Media.

Goulding, M., Barthem, R., & Ferreira, E.J.G. (2003). *Atlas of the Amazon.* Smithsonian Books.

Granna. (2014). *Dzika Amazonia [Wild Amazon]* [puzzle game].

Guerra, C. (2015). *El Abrazo de la Serpiente (Embrace of the Serpent)* [film]. Colombia. Ciudad Lunar Producciones. Length: 125 minutes.

Guerra, C. (2019a). *Green Frontier: Limited Series (Behind the Scenes).* Netflix.

Guerra, C. (2019b). *Frontera Verde* [Netflix streaming series]. Colombia. Dynamo. Length: N/A.

Hussey, C. (2005). *The Valley of Secrets.* Hodder Children's Books.

Ibbotson, E. (2014). *Journey to the River Sea.* MacMillan Children's Books.

Kann, D. (2019, February 9). Record Levels of Gold Mining are Destroying One of the Most Biodiverse Places on Earth, Study Shows. *CNN*. https://edition.cnn.com/2019/02/08/world/gold-mining-deforestation-peru-record-levels-trnd/index.html (accessed 20.02.2024).

Kawa, N.C. (2016). *Amazonia in the Anthropocene: People, Soils, Plants, Forests.* University of Texas Press.

Khoury, J. (2012). *Origin.* Penguin Group.

Kimerling, J. (1991). *Amazon Crude.* Natural Resource Defense Council.

Kohn, E. (2013). *How Forests Think: Toward an Anthropology Beyond the Human.* University of California Press.

Lanly, J.-P. (2003). *Deforestation and Forest Degradation Factors* [presentation]. XII Forestry Congress, Quebec City, Canada. http://www.fao.org/3/xii/ms12a-e.htm.

London, M., & Kelly, B. (2007). *The Last Forest: The Amazon in the Age of Globalization*. Random House.

McLean, G. (2017). *Jungle* [film]. Australia. Blumhouse Productions. Length: 115 minutes.

Meggers, B. (1954). Environmental Limitations on the Development of Culture. *American Anthropologist*, 56, 801–824.

Mitchell, S., & McLennan, C. (2007). *The Rainforest Grew All Around*. Sylvan Dell Publishing.

Nawrocka, E. (2010). *Opowieści o Raju utraconym: Przemiany topiki Raju w hispanoamerykańskiej powieści o selwie*. Wydawnictwo Uniwersytetu Jagiellońskiego.

Ortiz, V. (2007). *Legends of the Amazonas*. Abya Yala.

Patchett, A. (2011). *State of Wonder*. Bloomsbury.

Plotkin, M.J. (1993). *Tales of a Shaman's Apprentice: An Ethnobotanist Searches for New Medicines in the Amazon Rain Forest*. Penguin Books.

Rangel, A. (1920). *Inferno verde: Cenas y cenários do Amazonas*. T.E. Arrault. (first issue: 1908).

Rival, L. (2016). *Huaorani Transformations in Twenty-first-century Ecuador: Treks into the Future of Time*. The University of Arizona Press.

Rivera, J.E. (1924). *La Vorágine*. Luis Tamayo y Cia.

Rollins, J. (2002). *Amazonia*. William Morrow.

Romero, S., & Krauss, C. (2011). Ecuador's Judge Orders Chevron to Pay $9 Billion. *New York Times*. http://www.nytimes.com/2011/02/15/world/americas/15ecuador.html?_r=0.

Roth, E. (2013). *Green Inferno* [film]. USA-Chile. Blumhouse Productions. Length: 100 minutes.

Rundell, K. (2017). *The Explorer*. Bloomsbury.

Schwartzman, S., & Zimmerman, B. (2005). Conservation Alliances with Indigenous Peoples of the Amazon. *Conservation Biology*, 3(19), 721–727.

Shakespeare, W. (2004). *The Tempest*. Washington Square Press Inc.

Smith, N.J.H. (1999). *The Amazon River Forest: A Natural History of Plants, Animals, and People*. Oxford University Press.

Sobich-Kamińska, A. (2017). *Odkrywcy. Amazonia*. Wydawnictwo Zielona Sowa.

Taj, M. (2019). Peru Launch Crackdown on Illegal Gold Mining in Amazon. *Reuters*, 20 February. https://www.reuters.com/article/us-peru-illegal-mining/peru-launches-crackdown-on-illegal-gold-mining-in-amazon-id USKCN1Q82U6?feedType=RSS&feedName=environmentNews (accessed 31.07.2019).

Thacker, N. (2016). *The Amazon Code* (Kindle edition). Turtleshell Press.

Watts, J. (2018, January 10). New Round of Oil Drilling Goes Deeper into Ecuador's Yasuni National Park. *The Guardian*. https://www.theguardian.com/environment/2018/jan/10/new-round-of-oil-drilling-goes-deeper-into-ecuadors-yasuni-national-park.

Wechterowicz, P. (2012). *Śnieżek i Węgielek. Podróż do Amazonii.* Wydawnictwo Alegoria Sp. z o.o.
Wicks, B. (2018). *Tempted by Her Hot-Shot Doc.* Harlequin Mills & Boon Limited.
Worth, B. (2003). *If I Ran the Rainforest.* Dr. Seuss Enterprises, Random House.
WWF. (2014). https://www.worldwildlife.org/stories/protecting-the-amazon-for-life (accessed 20.02.2024).

5 Conclusions

At the beginning of the 21st century, two significant popular science works emerged – "Postcolonialism: A Very Short Introduction" by Robert J.C. Young (2003) and "Decolonization: A Very Short Introduction" by Dane Kennedy (2016). Both books are part of the "Very Short Introductions" series published by Oxford University Press, which includes over 600 titles aimed at providing readers with accessible insights into basic contemporary issues. These publications are of a popular science nature, and their authors are scholars associated with Oxford University. The "Very Short Introductions" series shapes common opinions on crucial matters such as history, art, politics, and philosophical and social thought in an accessible manner.

In Kennedy's definition, decolonization is the "fall of colonial empires and the creation of new nation-states across what came to be known in the decades following World War II as the Third World" (Kennedy 2016: 5). The author discusses four successive historical waves of decolonization. The first wave began in the 17th century with the rebellion of settlers in North America against British rule and lasted the beginning of the 19th century when South American countries gained their independence. Kennedy notes that this was accompanied by violence and bloodshed, influencing the later fate of these countries. The second wave of decolonization took place in Europe, initiated by the outbreak of World War I and the fall of the Russian Empire. Kennedy places its boundary in the 1920s when newly formed European states grappled with ethnic and religious issues. The main, third wave of decolonization occurred after World War II when areas later called the Third World liberated themselves from European colonial rule. This process lasted for 30 years, resulting in the creation of over a hundred new countries (Kennedy 2016: 46). Kennedy recounts the history of colonial wars and local uprisings that led to changes almost worldwide. Some new nation-states triumphed, while others faced dramatic problems. The fourth wave of decolonization encompasses several places worldwide as it refers to the period after 1989 when Eastern and Central European countries rejected Soviet dominance, leading to the disintegration of this empire. Kennedy rhetorically concludes his introduction to decolonization by asking whether the fall of the greatest

DOI: 10.4324/9781003495055-5

contemporary empire, the United States, will lead to another, fifth wave of decolonization.

The author of the second mentioned publication, R. Young, discusses postcolonialism, perceiving it as the "ways in which the relations between western and non-western people and their worlds are viewed" (Young 2003: 2). The path to this involves developing theoretical structures that would enable a perception of the world different from the "Western" one. The author emphasizes that postcolonialism, as a trend, is not uniform, and it is challenging to formulate a specific theoretical thought because each implements postcolonialism in its way and to varying degrees. The idea of postcolonialism in this context is to recognize and acknowledge other ways of viewing the world. Young's book takes the reader through various events that he considers results of postcolonial actions, although, as he emphasizes, these are often events concerning people "invisible" in the discourse led by the West because the Western world does not perceive issues beyond its way of thinking. As Young writes, the postcolonial process is the translation "from the disempowered to the empowered" (Young 2003: 8). An essential element on this path is minority knowledge, which should be treated in the Western world as seriously as Western knowledge – a valid demand, though somewhat utopian in times when all minorities are dominated by the scientific and moral achievements of the West.

I mention these two positions because they address important cultural and social issues, and they are directed at a broad audience. They show decolonization and postcolonialism in various forms and examples from different parts of the world. However, for the Indigenous inhabitants of the Amazon, there is not much space in them: Kennedy discusses the process of gaining independence by former colonies of Spain and Portugal, but the Amazon Indigenous peoples are not present in it, and Young, when describing grassroots postcolonial movements in Brazil, devotes only one sentence to Indigenous groups. Remaining invisible in the discourse on decolonization and postcolonialism speaks to the persistence of understanding Amazon Indigenous peoples as entirely different from what is commonly accepted in Western culture. Therefore, what needs to be done is symbolic decolonization and a real postcolonial approach in the discourse on these Indigenous groups. Due to the actual lack of starting this process in Western culture, the image presented in cultural texts has remained unchanged for decades.

Amazonia and its inhabitants, as a geographically and culturally distant world, are usually depicted in contemporary cultural texts in a somewhat stereotypical way and are typically framed within the boundaries of otherness. Exoticism (and exoticization) invariably forms part of the Western gaze because, in the concept of Western culture, the Amazon still remains something mysterious, incomprehensible, distant in space and time. There is probably no other area that is equally fascinating but also fear-inducing. Therefore, an external view must remain within the framework of amazement. Even documentary forms do not avoid this; for example, a National Geographic documentary (NG 2016) showing the "wild Amazon" and narrating the tropical forest's story also presents its inhabitants (in this case, the Matsés). However, it does so in the form of the noble savage, dressing them in traditional costumes and portraying as knowledgeable about the secrets of the forest. At one point, the film introduces the phrase "unlike the plant-cutter ants . . ., the Matsés never relied on gardening" (NG 2016, 00:19:26) placing the forest's inhabitants in a somewhat awkward position concerning the understanding of their cultural practices. This documentary is not an exception. An image using the category of "otherness" is not created exclusively in the arts such as literature, film, games, or photography, as it is based on a certain fixed cultural narrative. An Indigenous person must "look like an Indian" to be credible – hence even travel books or journalistic reports exploit such an image of Amazon inhabitants. As Marcin Gawrycki (2010) writes during the analysis of Polish travel literature, travelers experience Latin America and describe it as "different" already beyond their doorstep, so the stereotypical image is inevitable. Almost all the texts analyzed by the author sin with the titular "chase for imagination", seeking what is expected and anticipated, so that is precisely what they find. And we are talking here about authors of texts that are, by definition, non-fictional – hence it is not difficult to understand how much leeway authors of films or fictional books can have, who are not held accountable for the "truth" of presented facts.

In the chapter discussing the concept of exoticism and exoticization, among others, I quoted the words of Bruce Kapferer and Dimitrios Theodossopoulos, stating that exoticization romanticizes, patronizes, and caricatures the elements being presented (Kapferer and Theodossopoulos 2016: 19) – it seems that these three terms encompass almost all the cultural texts analyzed here. As a result, three ways of presenting the Indigenous inhabitants of the Amazon emerge: we see them as noble savages, living in harmony with nature; as "savages" who cannot create a "higher" culture; or as possessors of the truth about the world and humans, deep knowledge related to nature. The issue of caricaturing also finds its place in cultural texts, especially when, in a distorted mirror, they portray some cultural practices, such as anthropophagy transformed into cannibalism or elements of shamanism shown as a neo-shamanistic quest for visions.

Cultural texts written from the perspective of Western culture do not address topics significant from the point of view of the Amazon inhabitants themselves, and from this fact, two observations arise: first, the presented image of the inhabitants of the Amazon is "naive" or "wild", perhaps because our thinking about them does not go beyond stereotypes. Second, crimes committed during the colonization period do not even allow for a broader reflection on the situation of Amazonian Indigenous groups because it would require confronting the dimensions of what happened over almost 500 years. Are these the reasons for the persistence of the image of the Amazonian

Conclusions 107

Figure 5.1 Frequency distribution of various images of Indigenous inhabitants in analyzed cultural texts. The analysis reveals a predominance of stereotypical images of Indigenous inhabitants in the examined cultural texts, encompassing idealized, violent, magical, and historically stagnant portrayals.

"other"? Or, approaching the matter from a different perspective, does the distance and cultural distinctiveness simply prevent artists from going beyond the confines of popular thinking? (see Figure 5.1)

Another thread that could potentially lead to finding an answer to the treatment of Amazon inhabitants in cultural texts as "wild" or "innocent" or "possessing secret knowledge of life" is the misunderstanding of various cultural aspects by people from outside the Amazon, and more precisely, even outside a particular culture. We are writing about practices that we can describe, that we notice, and based on this, we often draw further conclusions about how people function and perceive the world. In recent years, studies on the Amazon have focused on the relationships between what is human and what is not human, including the relationships of each person with the animal and plant world, with the environment of which a given person is a part. The term that comes closest to these meanings is "anti-essentialist neoliberalism" which attempts to understand the world as a network of relationships between different beings (Ogden et al. 2013: 6). Western cultural texts do not have much to say about cultural practices in the Amazon (in their true form), so there can be no place for connections with the "non-human" world in them. The concept itself is so foreign to Western culture that recipients would probably often react with incomprehension or ridicule (which would not be a particularly new reaction).

Returning to the question of why the inhabitants of the tropical forest remain "strangers" another argument could be mentioned: in the concept of representatives of Western culture, the Amazon is a place where practically anything can happen. Therefore, it is easy to exploit its natural resources – including human resources – because local residents are often presented as part of the forest, placing the action and characters in a place with so many different possibilities.

At this point, it would be appropriate to ask how the Indigenous inhabitants of the Amazon should be presented to avoid their exoticization. Certainly, this issue does not concern only art in a broad sense but also our general thinking about ethnic groups in this region. Documentary programs and reports, as mentioned above, often replicate stereotypes or, under the guise of "fact" show staged scenes to confirm stereotypical image, so they cannot be very reliable sources of information. There are really few cultural texts conveying a realistic picture of cultural practices in the Amazon, and they are united by the fact that they show everyday life without emphasizing everything that is "different". Interestingly, books for children and young adult novels exhibit the most of these characteristics, giving hope that the image emerging from them will be devoid of exoticism and will only arouse friendly curiosity among young readers to know more. On the other hand, perhaps we need more works like "La terra degli uomini rossi" (Bechis 2008), which talk about the contemporary everyday life of Indigenous inhabitants and present them as ordinary people. However, this film did not reach a wide audience, however it was shown at festivals and received the One World Media award (Cooper 2016), but it did not resonate loudly in more popular media. Cultural texts like this last one should be more widespread – depicting the ordinary life of Indigenous inhabitants of the Amazon without exoticism, without emphasizing alleged naivety, incompetence, or "wildness". Showing them as ordinary people with whom we can share concerns and joys, regardless of where in the world we come from.

References

Bechis, M. (2008). *La terra degli uomini rossi (Birdwatchers)* [film]. Brazil. Lilt Films. Length: 104 minutes.

Cooper, S. (2016). https://www.screendaily.com/bechis-honoured-at-one-world-media-awards-/5015312.article (accessed 20.03.2024).

Gawrycki, M.F. (2010). *W pogoni za wyobrażeniami. Próba interpretacji polskiej literatury podróżniczej poświęconej Ameryce Łacińskiej*. Wydawnictwo Uniwersytetu Warszawskiego.

Kapferer, B., & Theodossopoulos, D. (eds.). (2016). *Against Exoticism: Toward the Transcendence of Relativism and Universalism in Anthropology*. Berghahn.

Kennedy, D. (2016). *Decolonization. A Very Short Introduction*. Oxford University Press.

NG. (2016). *Wild Amazon*. National Geographic.

Ogden, L., Hall, B., & Tanita, K. (2013). Animals, Plants, People and Things: A Review of Multispecies Ethnography. *Environment and Society*, 4, 5–24.

Young, R.J.C (2003). *Postcolonialism. A Very Short Introduction*. Oxford University Press.

Index

Abad Espinoza, Louis Gregorio 88
Aché-Guayaki, ethnic group 74
Acuña, Cristóbal de 9, 16n4, 91
Akawaio, ethnic group 48
Albert, Bruce 15, 26, 28
Allende, Isabel 27, 28, 63, 76, 81, 94
Andoke, ethnic group 40
Andoke, language 39
Andujar, Claudia 29–30
Arana Julio César 38–39
Arens, William 73
Arnold, Jack 14
Asch, Timothy 14
Attenborough, David, Sir 28

Babb, Florence E. 79
Barasano, ethnic group 65
Barnard, Alan 10
Basso, Ellen 21–22
Bates, Henry W. 11, 12, 43, 44, 91
Bechis, Marco 83, 108
Berg, Peter 80, 98
Besette, Christopher M. 25, 61, 62, 76
Biet, Antoine 57
Black, Samantha 69
Bodley, John 15
Boorman John 14
Bora, ethnic group 40
Bora, language 39
Borofsky, Robert 15, 27
Brown, Michael F. 57
Brown, Paula 23
Buryats, ethnic group 54

Cadaval, Leonardo 83
Carvajal, Gaspar de 8, 9, 16n2
Casement, Roger 38–40, 48n3, 81
Castaneda, Carlos 58–59, 69
Chagnon, Napoleon 14, 15, 16, 25, 26, 27, 28, 81
Cherry, Lynn 60, 93
Chico, Mendes *see* Filho, Francico Alves Mendes
Chołaj, Henryk 8, 12
Columbus, Christopher 7, 12, 73, 91
Conklin, Beth 74, 75
Cook, James 9
Countinho J. 60
Crouch, David 1
Cubeo, ethnic group 42
Cunha, Euclides da 92

D'Amato, Joe 75
Davis, Shelton H. 15
Davis, Wade 88
Defoe, Daniel 10
de las Casas, Bartolomé 9, 16n1, 39, 9
Deodato, Rugger 75
Devereux, George 58
Doyle, Arthur Conan 14
Dryden, John 1
Dutilleux, Jean Pierre 46, 82, 84

Echeverri, Juan Alvaro 39, 40
Eliade, Mircea 58
Elizondo, Gabriel 81
Elliot, Elisabeth 36
Enawene Nawe, ethnic group 38

Ese Eja, ethnic group 41
Evenk, ethnic group 54

Fausto, Carlos 56, 74
Fawcett, Percival Harrison 19–22, 76
Filho, Francico Alves Mendes 82
Finer, Matt 90
Fisher, Philip 82
Flores, Franklin Ayala 20
Forsyth, Adrian 88
Frisch, Albert 13

Gaiman, Neil 22
Gawrycki, Marcin 106
Geruzel, Ewa 94
Ghinsberg, Jossie 98
Goffin, Alvin M. 34
Goodyear, Charles 89
Goulding, Michael 89
Gow, Peter 4, 56, 74
Grann, David 19, 22
Greenwood, Davyd J. 15, 78
Guarani, ethnic group 45, 46, 74, 83
Guerra, Cirro 40, 41, 42, 46, 47, 64, 65, 84, 95, 98

Hamburger, Cao 45
Hanon, Jim 35, 36
Harner, Michael 66, 67
Hemming, John 8, 9, 10, 11, 22, 45, 46
Hergé 22
Heritage, Paul 82, 83
Herzog, Werner 14
Hoyt, Harry O. 14
Huaorani, ethnic group 22, 34–38, 41, 48n1, 54–55, 65, 78, 88
Huao terero, language 34, 35
Humboldt, Alexander von 9, 12
Hussey, Charmian 43, 44, 66, 81, 98
Hutchins, Frank 15, 78, 79

Ibbotson, Eve 44, 95
Ingarikó, ethnic group 48, 80

Jacob, Frank 74
Juruna, ethnic group 74

Kaiabi, ethnic group 45
Kakutani, Michiko 19
Kalapalo, ethnic group 21, 45
Kann, Drew 90
Kamaiurá, ethnic group 46, 82
Kapferer, Bruce 6, 106
Karapano, ethnic group 42
Kawa, Nicholas C. 87, 88
Kayapó, ethnic group 23
Kenin-Lopsan, Mongush B. 54
Kennedy, Dane 104–105
Khoury, Jessica 44, 45, 97
Kimerling, Judith 90
Koch-Grünberg, Theodore 40, 41, 42
Kohn, Eduardo 87, 88
Kopenawa, Davi 28, 29, 62
Kranstover, Grace 79
Krutak, Lars 45
Kuczyński, Maciej 66–68
Kuligowski, Waldemar 73

Lanly, Jean-Paul 89
Leopold II 38
Leopoldine 10
Lery, Jean de 9, 10
Lippmann, Walter 4
Llosa, Luis 14
Llosa, Mario Vargas 38–40
London, Mark 91
Lóránt, Attila 37–38
Louis, William Roger 38
Luna, Luis Eduardo 69

Machiguenga, ethnic group 37, 38
Mackie, Diane M. 4
Manara, Milo 31
Manchineri, ethnic group 65
Margheriti, Antonio 75
Markham, Clements C. 16n1
Marshal, John 14
Martinez-Gugerli, Kristen 78
Martius, C.F.P. von 11
Mashco-Piro, ethnic group 79
Maya, ethnic group 69, 99
McGarthy, Craig 5
Medici, Lorenzo Pietro Francesco di 8

Meggers, Betty 87
Mitchell, Susan 93
Moipa 35, 48n1
Montaigne, Michel de 10
Moore Thomas 10
Muinane, ethnic group 40
Muinane, language 39

Narby, Jeremy 57
Navarro, Barbara 30–31, 64, 84
Nawrocka, Ewa 91
Neel, James 81
Nelson, Jimmy 37
Nonuya, ethnic group 40
Nugent, Stephen 7, 13, 14

Oakes, Tim 79
Ocaina, ethnic group 39, 40, 42
Ogden, Laura 27, 107
Olivares, Gerardo 29
Orellana, Francisco de 8
Ortiz, Vinicio 93
Oviedo, Fernandez de 57
Oxford, Pete 37

Panoan, linguistic group 74
Patamona, ethnic group 48
Patchett, Ann 33, 34, 97
Peluso, Daniela 41
Platt, Richard 60, 79
Plotkin, Mark 60, 61, 89

Quichua, ethnic group 22, 37, 65, 67

Rabelais, François 10
Raleigh, Walter 28
Ramos, Alcida 15, 26, 61
Rangel, Alberto 91–92
Rival, Laura 87, 88, 89
Rivera, José 92
Roe, Peter G. 65
Rollins, James 31–33, 64, 96–97
Romero, Simon 90
Roth, Eli 75, 96
Ruby, Jay 13–14
Ruffino, Mauro Luis 48n4
Runa, ethnic group 54, 55
Rundell, Katherine 44, 95, 99

Said, Edward 5
Saint, Nate 36
Saint, Rachel 34
Schultes, Richard Evans 34, 40–42, 43, 44, 65
Schwartzman, Stephan 90
Scott, Katie 2
Seuss, Dr. 93
Shipaya, ethnic group 74
Shuar, ethnic group 22, 33, 55, 67, 88
Siriano, ethnic group 42
Smith, Nigel 89
Sobich-Kamińska Anna 94
Spix, Johann B. von 11
Sponsel, Leslie 15
Spruce, Richard 11, 12, 43, 57
Staden, Hans 73
Sting 2, 28
Stoff, Andrzej 5

Taylor, Kenneth 15, 26
Teevan, Colin 82
Teixeira, Pedro 9, 91
Thacker, Nick 33, 95, 97
Theodossopoulos, Dimitrios 6, 106
Thurn, Everard im 12–14
Todorov, Tzvetan 7
Tupi-Guarani, ethnic group 45, 46
Tupi-Guarani, linguistic group 44
Tupinambá, ethnic group 9, 10, 73, 74
Turner, Terence 15

Urry, John 15, 78

Vaz de Caminha, Pêro 9, 16n5
Veron, Marcos 83
Vespucci, Amerigo 8, 16n1, 73
Vilaça, Aprecida 74
Villas Boas, brothers 45
Vitebsky, Piers 54, 55, 56
Voltaire 10

Walker, Alice 68–69
Wallace, Alfred R. 11–12, 43, 44
Wallace, Tim 78

Wallis, Robert 58
Walsh, Roger 58
Wari', ethnic group 74
Waters, Roger 2
Watson, Fiona 26
Watts, Jonathan 90
Wayapí, ethnic group 44
Wechterowicz, Przemysław 94
Whitehead, Neal 7, 57
Whitten, Norman 23, 54, 55, 59
Wicks, Betty 48, 80, 99
Wied-Neuwied, Maximilian zu 10
Wierucka, Aleksandra 34–37, 42, 54, 55, 60, 65, 78, 79
Witoto, ethnic group 39, 40, 42, 47

Witoto, language family 39
Worth, Bonnie 93

Xingu, ethnic group 66

Yagua, ethnic group 40
Yaminahua, ethnic group 37
Yanomami, ethnic group 15, 16, 19, 23–33, 44, 55, 60–64, 74–75, 76, 81, 83–84
Yost, James 36, 63
Young, Robert J.C. 104–105

Ziegler-Otero, Lawrence 34
Żygulski, Zdzisław 5

For Product Safety Concerns and Information please contact our EU
representative GPSR@taylorandfrancis.com
Taylor & Francis Verlag GmbH, Kaufingerstraße 24, 80331 München, Germany

www.ingramcontent.com/pod-product-compliance
Lightning Source LLC
Chambersburg PA
CBHW051756230426
43670CB00012B/2307